Cultural Crossroads

Cultural Crossroads

A Roadmap for Successful
Global Relocation

Ann D. Clark, PhD

iUniverse®

CULTURAL CROSSROADS
A ROADMAP FOR SUCCESSFUL GLOBAL RELOCATION

iUniverse books may be ordered through booksellers or by contacting:

iUniverse
1663 Liberty Drive
Bloomington, IN 47403
www.iuniverse.com
1-800-Authors (1-800-288-4677)

ISBN: 978-1-4917-8478-5 (sc)
ISBN: 978-1-4917-8480-8 (hc)
ISBN: 978-1-4917-8479-2 (e)

Library of Congress Control Number: 2015920292

Print information available on the last page.

iUniverse rev. date: 03/04/2016

Dedication

To the employees of ACI Specialty Benefits--past, present and future--who have helped create a living legacy that has changed the lives of thousands across the globe.

Contents

Acknowledgements

Although this book contains over 50,000 words, there are never enough to thank the many who have generously given time, support, and encouragement. First, to Adora Luster, whose creativity and criticism helped hone the final form, heartfelt appreciation. Aaron Grisafi, *Graphic Artist Extraordinaire*, skillfully and beautifully created the outstanding cover. To Deanna Smith, whose diligence in reading, developing, organizing and editing made this book real, sincere thanks. To the many interviewees, bosses and employees alike, thank you for the generous gift of personal stories, time, and insights. To the corporations that have contributed to the ideas in the book, to the great employees who work there, and to the families who support them, thank you all.

About ACI

ACI Specialty Benefits ranks in the nation's Top-Ten providers of employee assistance programs (EAP), corporate wellness, student assistance, concierge, and work/life services to corporations worldwide. With a 95 percent client retention rate and over seven million covered lives, ACI has provided personalized, high-touch service to clients for over thirty years. For the latest in benefits innovation, check out MacroLife – The Game of Benefits at www.acispecialtybenefits.com/macrolife. For information about ACI's global resources and services, visit www.acispecialtybenefits.com/international.

Preface

My first trip out of the country was to Canada. My father, an ardent fisherman and cheapskate, insisted on camping, cooking, and following military rules outdoors. That, added to bug spray, mosquitoes, no swimming in the unknown waters plus warnings about the horrors of the forest, should have made me never want to leave home again. But Juarez beckoned. A high school trip led me to learn a whole new vocabulary (it was the same in English as in Spanish) and created an all-consuming curiosity about what went on in these darkened bars that swarthy men beckoned us into. Exhilarating for a teenager, but again, not a reason to leave home.

Luckily, a trip to Spain via London and Paris was my next step. The romance of all the history books and novels was coming true. Landing at the fabled Heathrow made up for the various delays, bus rides and tourist complaints. I fell in love with the sights, sounds – and I truly embraced discomfort – because they were often such eye-opening experiences. The first thing I learned is that Europeans, and what Americans call foreigners, are much better informed about America than are Americans. I was asked political questions that were astute, current and erudite. And for most, I had rather superficial answers. Furthermore, most everyone speaks more than one language. How narrow and hypocritical that Americans insist on only one! To find a shopkeeper who could sell in more than six languages and a tour guide that spouted more American history than I knew…well, I was hooked.

My travels have now included countries on many continents, tourist and out-of-the-way destinations, and a constant marveling at how so many people have cultures, families, values, ingenuity, compassion and respect that are so much more genuine that what I see in my home country. Yes, it was fun to ride a camel and cruise the Nile on a barge like Cleopatra. Yes, it was fun to eat foods I could not identify and entertain street vendors. Yes, it was weird to have my red hair touched by hordes of Taiwanese who had never seen such.

Mostly, I became a better person, with a world view that was enlarged, a cultural sensitivity that badly needed broadening and a new interest in the global politics about which America is so ignorant. And I had fun! I made friends for life and had once-in-a-lifetime experiences. I hope this book will provide both practical and uplifting insights for expats and others who are lucky and smart enough to push the borders, endure discomfort and open up to new horizons—in the form of meeting people, seeing places and having adventures.

I am also proud to say that my grandchildren – Bellamy, with months in Paris, Cuba and more, Ian and Jordan already bi-literate with immersion schooling, and Zachary, a devoted cruiser – have inherited or learned my love of travel and adventure. Bellamy and I spent last Christmas in Buenos Aires and I am already planning my next trip! (Maybe she is…)

Happy trails to you, reader and, I hope, fellow traveler.

Introduction

"The world is a book and those who do
not travel read only one page."
– St. Augustine

Spin a globe, close your eyes and pick a spot – American business is there. That business takes the form of workers – from oil riggers and mining engineers, to language specialists, administrative assistants, accountants and nurses. Name a job, and there is worldwide demand. These people selected to work abroad are called expatriates. This book is about the adjustments that individuals and families will need to make when choosing to relocate to another country, and the impact those factors will have in the workplace and at home, wherever home may be for the expatriate.

Corporations send people around the world and, like anyone, expatriates have lives of increasing complexity. Just as at home in the United States, there is always a new cell phone to buy, an organic miracle food to order, a babysitter to hire, a dog to walk, a car to service, and even a piano to be tuned. The myriad tasks that make up the daily lives of most people can seem routine or even mundane. But picture those same tasks being performed in Hong Kong, Barcelona, Buenos Aires or Seoul and the picture changes radically. Language and cultural barriers can add new dimensions of difficulty to previously simple chores. No matter where you are in the world, you will need to provide food, shelter and transportation for yourself and your family, and even those basics can become frustrating and challenging without sufficient guidance and support.

Companies are transporting American workers to places where business and markets are surging. An estimated 6.3 million Americans[1] are now living outside the United States and that number climbs every year. The demand for personnel at all levels means that the expatriate population is itself a growing industry. In a survey conducted by the Society for Human Resources Management (SHRM), an international human resources association, 39% of participants indicated using "alternative international assignments," and 23% are planning to expand expatriate presence in the near future[2]. Also referred to as "global transfer," 57% of multinational companies were expected to increase the number of employees outside their home countries in 2013, and 37 percent planned to sustain existing rates of global relocation[3]. The expatriate has become a well-accepted and growing segment of the workforce.

These growing changes in corporate cultures and global economics present unique challenges. Sara Judy, Corporate Business Manager for *Suite America*, says, "Cost savings with relocation to Asia and India are undeniable. Economic realities and cost efficiencies are often not a choice for corporate America, rather a necessity. The cost benefits offset the relocation of experts to work, train and manage workforces abroad." As global expansion increases, businesses must create processes for moving into new markets, and establish infrastructure abroad to support their international growth.

The Changing Face of the Expatriate Worker

Who are these American expatriates? Expatriates are defined, for the purposes of this book, as Americans living and working abroad in a culture other than their own. Usually, expats are connected to a

---

1 Winn, "Are expats…?"

2 Society, "SHRM's 2012."

3 Cartus, "2012 Trends."

corporate entity, but many go as contracted or independent workers. *Cultural Crossroads* specifically addresses corporate America and its expatriate workforce, but the processes outlined here can also help students or retirees contemplating a move abroad.

What does an expatriate look like? There are more men than women, although studies show a recent increase from 9 to 20 percent in the number of women going abroad to live and work. Expatriates tend to be more highly educated than the average employee in either their homeland or new location. Expats also tend to be younger. In fact, the age of the average expatriate is dropping. In the last year, 41 percent of the expatriate workforce was between 20 and 39 years old. Recently that figure jumped 13 percent, meaning 54 percent of the global expatriate workforce falls between the ages of 20 and 39.

Expatriates also tend to earn more money, enabling hired staff, private schools and larger homes to become affordable. These necessary and far from luxury services are just a few of the perks that go along with relocation. Expats may live in exotic and upscale cosmopolitan cities, and take interesting cultural excursions and vacations during their stays. This is the type of lifestyle that attracts corporate workers to accept positions abroad.

Expatriates can be single, a married couple, or a family with children. They will likely be experienced corporate employees who have been with the organization for several years, long enough to earn the trust and respect required to assume the responsibilities of acting as a company representative abroad. They may speak a second language, or have experiences living, working or studying abroad that make them good candidates. Expatriates working abroad will need to have excellent organizational, leadership and communication skills, and be highly adaptable and creative. Expatriates should be adept at project management, and be able to complete long-term goals and commitments.

Dreaming of an International Lifestyle

Your boss announces that you and your family will be living abroad for two years in Oman. This desirable, oil-rich country combined with corporate incentives provides a lavish lifestyle. Friends and family are excited and a little envious. Your family is hopeful about the many opportunities such an assignment will provide. Dreams of housekeepers, luxurious homes, free travel and more become real. You'll be escaping from the sometimes dull nature of ordinary life. Isn't this an increasingly shared fantasy of individuals across the world? Don't we all have visions of sandy beaches with swaying palms; tall spires topping cobblestone streets; quaint villages and sweeping architecture untarnished by traffic and poverty? New horizons beckon, suggesting adventure and excitement, and for the select few being offered a corporate transfer, the dream of moving abroad may become a reality.

Most Americans moving abroad look forward to a warm welcome from their host country. Bienvenido a Espana! Willkommen in Deutschland! Bienvenue en France! Benvenuti in Italia! As a U.S. citizen moving to a foreign country, you may anticipate being invited into a local's home, being treated like long-lost family, trying delicious new foods in a quaint and comfortable setting, being the center of attention and interest, trying out a few words of the native language and receiving appreciative nods and chuckles. However, the reality could include lonely nights in a hotel room, confusing menus, difficulties communicating, and frustration in trying to accomplish the most basic things, like eating, drinking, getting to and from your destination, and paying for things.

The chance to change one's life is a thrilling challenge and the act of making a go of it abroad can lead to all sorts of new opportunities. But for many people, becoming an expatriate and an international citizen is not all it's cracked up to be. The rising attrition rate among expats suggests trouble in paradise. Why do some people love living abroad while others return home with cynical and depressing memories of the experience? Is it a case of integration issues or culture shock? Is the expatriate dream a reality or a myth? Are the reasons employees expatriate purely money-orientated? Corporations want answers, and a process to put in place to increase the candidate's chances for success.

Cultural Crossroads provides companies and individuals with an easy-to-follow roadmap for success, to make global relocation easier, more profitable and ultimately successful. Author Dr. Ann Clark combines 30 years of providing corporate employee benefit service around the globe with her personal experiences as a world traveler, plus an abundance of stories of real people and their experiences, into a complete guide for future expatriates. The book offers corporations, individuals and families practical solutions to dilemmas faced by the increasing number of Americans living abroad. This book is about change, adaptation, assimilation, and learning from other expatriates. At the end of this reading, you will have all the information you need to make your decision about whether to become an expatriate, and you will have a five-part plan to make your global relocation successful.

Grow Where You are Transplanted

What allows some expatriates and families to thrive offshore, as opposed to others who embark on a failed assignment? A failed assignment is defined as a posting that either ends prematurely or is considered ineffective by senior management. Research into failed corporate postings finds that failure rates are high and can range from 10 to 70 percent depending on the country. Since business does not restrict itself to luxurious environments, corporate America has personnel needs in many developing countries, or those that have objectively lower living standards. Although the flexibility and mobility of the younger generation is changing the look of the American population in Europe, the majority of expatriates are still young couples or families sent on overseas assignments, usually lasting an average of three to four years.

"The relocation business has really changed in the last 10 years," stated Ms. Viv Hermans, a relocation expert. "I find that more young families are moving overseas."[4] Learning a foreign language is no longer optional, even in U.S. schools, and parents want their children to have a world view with more opportunities than they had. Nowadays college graduates may already have traveled abroad, maybe more than once, either studying abroad or for family vacations. Many parents want their children to become citizens of the world, and taking an expat assignment is a great opportunity to expose the family to the benefits of world travel.

And where are they going? Siberia isn't known as a vacation destination, yet vast amounts of natural resources, including all-important oil, are found there. Ken M. Burgess, international Employee Assistance Program (EAP) manager,[5] describes the various businesses that exist in Siberia. "It is like a much younger America," Dr. Burgess says. "A picture far-removed from Russian wolfhounds and frozen tundra." Burgess specializes in helping businesses in foreign countries adapt to the vast changes necessary to compete in the global marketplace. "Most of those changes," says Burgess, "begin with bringing in the right people."

Following is a list of popular countries for expatriates[6]:

---

[4] "Living in France."

[5] Mr. Burgess, A Certified Employee Assistance Professional (CEAP) has worked in the field since the mid-70s. As the EAP Manager for US Steel, Gulf Oil and Alcoa he has helped implement numerous family expatriate services and international EAPs.

[6] Poelzl, Volker, "Living Abroad: How to Choose the Country Best for You," *Transitions Abroad Magazine,* July/August 2006.

Popular Countries

Argentina: Very affordable; great cultural wealth and friendly people

Australia: Similar culture; English-speaking; popular with students; great travel destination; very friendly people

Brazil: Quite affordable; great cultural experience and a friendly people; economically and politically fairly stable; opportunities for students, English teachers, and professionals

Costa Rica: Close to the U.S.; sizable expatriate community for a small country; low cost of living; popular with students and retirees

Czech Republic: Among the cheaper destinations in Europe; friendly people, great history and culture

France: The classic destination for American expats and students, but relatively expensive

Italy: This is another classic destination for American expats; great culture and history

Japan: A popular destination for professionals and students from the U.S.; also popular with English teachers, but has very high cost of living and a very different culture and language

Mexico: Close to the U.S.; great culture and history and a friendly people; great for students, retirees, and English teachers

South Africa: Increasing economic and political stability; growing popularity with students; English speaking; great travel destination

Spain: Great cultural and historic wealth; popular destination with students; lower cost of living than in central or northern Europe

United Kingdom: The easiest and most popular destination for American expats because of the same language and similar culture

Anyone considering a move abroad should research their destination country in detail. Considerations such as safety, transportation, cleanliness, whether English is commonly spoken, proximity to America, weather, size, and even the availability of Starbucks can be deal breakers, or at least motivational factors.

Overcoming the Hurdles to Success

There are numerous challenges facing expatriates today. Predictably, surveys show that accommodations, language barriers, healthcare services, finances, making friends and finding schools top the list of expatriate problems. Corina G., whose husband moved offshore for a web design business, says, "We had many friends when we came to Thailand through both church and my husband's business. But we seem to have never discussed public schools or the lack thereof in Thailand. I guess I just thought my kids would go to the local Thai school and learn Thai by immersion." Corina's husband's employers didn't understand the situation and responded to the family's continuing requests for financial assistance by repeating, "Why can't they go to public schools?" Unfortunately for Corina, home schooling, tutoring and expensive private schools became a major dilemma.

What happens to those who fail? Repatriation, or failed assignments, cost corporations millions of dollars each year. The estimated cost of one executive relocation is as much as $2 million, and studies show that as many as 67 percent of expatriate postings fail. These numbers quickly hit the billion dollar mark for losses in American business.

Employees and families return early or are terminated for a wide variety of reasons. Individuals experience levels of cultural fatigue while others live in a state of denial, viewing the move as more of a "staycation" as opposed to a relocation. That billion dollar loss is passed on to all of us in the cost of goods and services. Do we really look at a smartphone and think of how much of that price is related to the success of expatriate work?

Relocation expert Sara Judy describes specific incidents of requests not uncommon to her industry. "Try locating a grand piano in Thailand," says Ms. Judy, "or musical instruments for an entire family." Unusual requests include an orthopedic dog bed, a $200 rice cooker and special haircuts. Her list is a long one. Companies like Judy's employer are in business to save that $2 million price tag for a failed relocation. While there is not a single answer to solving repatriation, there are many systems and resources that can significantly increase the success of the work and lives of expatriates.

A common problem is that expatriates often project an American lifestyle onto the offshore experience. Monique P., a young single woman with highly sought-after technical skills, says, "The foreign assignment seemed perfect to me. Being single, I saw it as an opportunity that I wouldn't have after marriage and children. But I was amazed at my own naiveté. I knew there wouldn't be shopping malls like in my native Redding, CA, but I had no idea of the crowds in the markets, the bartering and the difference in, well, cleanliness. I got used to blood in the gutters when I shopped at the butcher's kiosk. Ugh."

What is the main reason for expatriation failures? Often, proper planning – a seemingly simple part of placement – is missing. In the following chapters, you will find tools and techniques for a successful expatriate experience. Corporations will find strategic approaches to ensuring success for employees living abroad, that will ultimately contribute substantially to return on investment and the all-important bottom line. With literally billions of dollars at stake, the corporate investment in saving postings abroad is very high. With adequate hands-on resources and professional expertise, ***Cultural Crossroads*** will optimize every expatriate's opportunity for success.

Chapter One

Making the Decision - Do I Stay or Do I Go?

If your company is asking you to relocate to a foreign country, then you have a big decision to make. Can you pass up this opportunity of a lifetime? Are you the kind of person who can pull up stakes, leave your comfortable American home, familiar city, friends and family, and take up the challenge of living abroad? Will you accept the challenge of making your home away from the comforts of home?

Think of the challenges of moving within the United States, say to California or Wisconsin or Texas, and the cultural adjustments involved for you and your family, even just moving from the West Coast to the Southeast or Midwest. You will be dealing with different upbringings, values, school curriculums, home values, and activities. Now think of relocating to Germany, South Africa, or Peru, and the additional logistical issues when you throw in learning a new language, dealing with immigration officials, medical access, traveling long distances, cars and money. Are you up for it? Can you do it?

If you are reading this book, then you are on the right path. Researching this potential life change is the best way for you to evaluate your chances for success, or failure. Only you can decide what is best for you and your loved ones, and ***Cultural Crossroads*** will help you evaluate the factors that can assist you in making this life-changing determination.

Once granted the option to move abroad, many would-be expatriates are like juggernauts, ready for the experience. The excitement gets under their skin. This is the chance of a lifetime! Who wouldn't jump at the opportunity to go abroad – and get paid to do so?

Unlike the freedom of travel merely for brief work or vacation, expatriates will be making a new "nest." It may not be possible to visit the country before making the big move, but virtual resources can be good preparation. Scope out homes, taste the culture and imagine living abroad for an extended period of time. Create a virtual day and imagine that far from home.

As part of the research, keep a list of pros and cons updated as knowledge accumulates. As the cons list grows, consider solutions and resources to make the new country the best fit for you and your family. Move cons to the pros side as problems are solved with resources – virtual and real – in this new country.

"I had always wanted to travel the world," writes one expatriate, Marisa. "I wanted to see everything, but had chosen a more practical profession. So I was thrilled when my company offered me a promotion and a posting in Hong Kong! I accepted before even thinking about it, a decision I haven't regretted, but that came with its own issues that manifested all too quickly."

Take a breath. Sit down and begin planning out what toll the move could possibly have on your family, your career, and yourself. The move may bring about good changes – a chance at increased pay or promotion, a chance to experience a foreign country, a chance to introduce children to another language early on. But other changes might not be so simple. Deciding to move abroad requires a mindset beyond feelings. Preparation and logic should keep pace with feelings.

In addition to broadening horizons, living abroad also has many perks. Professionally speaking, living abroad looks great on a résumé. Living abroad, even for a short amount of time, shows adaptability, flexibility and that the employee can work well in a diverse environment. Problem solving is certainly a survival skill when living abroad. The list of positives can grow very long, very quickly.

Among the many challenging aspects, there are also many positives to immersion in a new place and culture. Jason M describes: "My first two weeks in Antwerp, Belgium, I wondered why everyone was treating me so coldly in the beautiful Flemish capital. On the other hand, I might have missed out on some of the more educational experiences of living my first year abroad if I had not rented a bargain apartment 200 meters from the 'red light' district. I wouldn't trade those strange stories for anything."

Is Expatriation the Right Choice for You?

Go through the following checklist and consider the answers in relation to your new assignment.

? Consider the Following

- ☐ **What are your short-term and long-term career goals? Do they line up with what is offered to you as an expatriate?**

  Moving abroad will take a significant amount of time, from anywhere between a few months to several years. If you and/or your family enjoy the country and get comfortable there, it might even be for a lifetime.

- ☐ **Is a move feasible? Will you have enough funds and support to live the life you expect to live in your new country?**

  Expatriates need financial planning. Be ready and prepared for changes in costs of living.

- ☐ **Are you embedded in American culture or are you interested in truly learning about how other cultures function?**

  Expatriates will experience many changes, from health and hygiene to language and religious practices that will seem strange and outlandish. Ensure you are ready to embrace and accept the challenge of change.

- ☐ **What is the effect on others if you relocate?**

  The choice to move does not lie on your shoulders or on those of your corporation alone. If you have a partner, children or both, discuss the opportunity with them and present it in a favorable light, with both pros and cons of what the move could mean. The least desirable thing is to ambush them or mislead them into having the wrong expectations.

Consider these items carefully and begin to share with friends and family. This choice is not just between the adventure of a lifetime or the comfort of your own home. Making choices involves comprehensive preparation and research. Working abroad can be an incredible experience that will broaden the individual's views of the world, provide a unique perspective on people and culture, and ultimately sparkle on a resume, declaring you to be a flexible, culturally-aware and risk-taking individual.

Do You Have What it Takes?

In order to make the expatriate assignment successful, organizations will use strategy and planning in the expatriate selection process. Employers may adopt comprehensive assessment instruments such as an International Assignment Profile (IAP) to select an ideal candidate for the particular assignment. Not every candidate is right for work abroad. Candidates must exhibit aptitude for flexibility and cultural awareness, and will represent the corporation for the next few months or years. The employee's personal success is crucial to the success of the expatriate assignment, so organizations are invested in that personal success.

Ask yourself these questions:

? Questions to Ask Yourself

- ☐ Do you make friends easily?
- ☐ How can you improve your social skills?
- ☐ Are you able to assimilate in an environment that may be drastically different from the one you are accustomed to?
- ☐ What is your style when forced to adapt?
- ☐ Are you multilingual? If not, are you excited to learn new languages and how quickly are you able to learn?
- ☐ Are you eager and curious to learn?
- ☐ Are you content with the fact that you may not be in control all the time?
- ☐ Are you relatively well-organized?
- ☐ Are you a problem-solver?
- ☐ Do you usually "go with the flow" when your plans abruptly change?
- ☐ Are you empathetic to others' thoughts and intentions, even strangers?
- ☐ Do you easily adapt to unusual or difficult situations?
- ☐ Do you like taking risks?
- ☐ Are you realistic about what situations you might be up against?
- ☐ Do you have the ability to laugh at yourself when you make mistakes?

Examine your answers. Assess realistically, with a plan for gaps and needed changes.

Sometimes sheer enthusiasm can be enough to change mindsets and needs. "I never thought of myself as a risk-taker," Bob L.

remembered when he returned from a two-year assignment in Costa Rica. "That's probably why I had such a hard time at first. But once I started to learn, I became more excited about what I was doing. I was more outgoing and naturally had to be more flexible once I got used to the Central American pace."

Characteristics of Successful Expatriates

- ✓ Positive attitude
- ✓ Open to learning
- ✓ Interested in life
- ✓ Social, outgoing
- ✓ Experience joy
- ✓ Supportive family
- ✓ Sturdy, healthy, hardy
- ✓ Busy, varied interests
- ✓ Goal directed
- ✓ Okay with risk
- ✓ Adventurous personality
- ✓ Work/life balance
- ✓ Resilient
- ✓ Flexible
- ✓ Philanthropic

If there are items on this list that do not describe you, think about how you might foster these abilities in yourself. If flexibility is not one of your assets, try to start with small stuff, making it a point to go with the flow a little more in your everyday life. If you are not philanthropic, get involved with a worthwhile cause. Small changes now can help change your mindset for your future expat life.

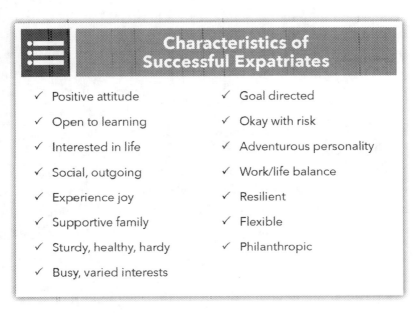

A best case scenario decision involves getting buy-in from everyone in the family, but of course that may not happen, especially if you have teenagers who are resistant to leaving their social network of friends. Communication is critical during the decision-making process. Change can be more difficult for some than others. But once the decision is made, acceptance is crucial. Jenny, the spouse of a sales executive being relocated to India, thought her children would be excited about their move abroad, but encountered tantrums and hostility. "We tried to get their agreement, but they weren't having any of it. I finally laid down the law and said 'This is what's going to happen, we are moving to Holland, and it is your choice whether you want to spend the next two years being miserable about it or enjoying it.' Once they realized this was a done deal, they became much more accepting and accommodating. We started to involve them in the process, showing them where their dad would be working, and some possible homes we might be living in, cities we could visit and trips we could take to other countries. It was hard for them to not get excited, once they accepted the decision had been made."

Once you decide to make the move, keep in mind, like any big decision, you may feel "buyer's remorse" or "cold feet". Mental resistance is to be expected. Keep moving forward in the direction you are going, making plans and lists, and try to put your doubts aside. You are bound for a great adventure, so don't let <u>you</u> hold you back!

Chapter Two

The 5 Stages for Successful Global Relocation

> "A journey of a thousand miles
> must begin with a single step."
> - Lao Tzu

Congratulations on your assignment abroad! It is a great opportunity, rarely offered by companies, and usually to their most valued and trusted employees. Consider it a vote of confidence that you have been asked to take on this role of "ambassador" for your company. You have the skills, and ***Cultural Crossroads*** will provide you with an easy-to-follow guide to get you there.

When relocating to a new country, expatriates and families generally experience five separate but interrelated stages of experiences.

> Stage 1: **Preparation.** How will expatriates be prepared to move? How can they tie up loose ends in one country and begin a new life in another? Is there a clearly defined strategy for the move? Preparation, research and preplanning are critical to the first phase.

Stage 2: **Transition.** What monetary, legal and work obstacles can expatriates expect to encounter as transitioning becomes real? Knowledge and research can help pave the way, and flexibility is an asset.

Stage 3: **Settling In.** How can expatriates lessen feelings of displacement? Will new friends be made? How can partners and family be ensured successful adaptation? The satisfaction of family members will be critical to the employee's ability to thrive.

Stage 4: **Adjustment.** How will expatriates deal with the inevitable culture shock? How does homesickness affect expatriate success? Will the language and cultural barriers hinder them from succeeding? Flexibility and a positive attitude will be helpful characteristics for the expatriate facing challenges in settling in to their new environment.

Stage 5: **Achieving Success.** How can success be achieved? Is happiness the measure? Experiences vary greatly, depending on an expatriate's circumstances and personality, the similarity of the host country to the home country and a wide number of variables that will influence success.

There is no 'average' expatriate experience from which to draw conclusions and solutions, but you may find similarities on which to base your template for success. Each individual's journey will vary, but these five stages provide a starting point. Each chapter in ***Cultural Crossroads*** has steps, tips, checklists and questions to guide your efficient integration abroad, and first-hand experiences to help prepare potential expats for a smooth, exciting and fulfilling settlement.

Stage 1: Preparation

"Do not follow where the path may lead. Go instead where there is no path and leave a trail."
- Ralph Waldo Emerson

Expatriates are far more likely to succeed in relocation with planning and help. Lack of planning can leave expatriates unable to find appropriate housing, scrambling to appease confused and upset children, and even barred from entering their destination country. Take advantage of corporate resources, including relocation and employee assistance services. Whether employees have selected the new location or the company has chosen it for them, a significant amount of research is required. Start with knowledge. Begin internet research. Read travel books. Consult travel-savvy friends. Create a file of expatriate resources from the internet. Seek out corporate expatriate trainings and additional resources.

Lorne K. remembers, "We got the cheapest moving company we could find. They quoted us a thousand dollars less than their competitors right over the phone. It couldn't be simpler! Well, when we got to Munich, our moving company said we couldn't get our belongings back until we paid an outrageously high tax. It was the worst possible situation: We were stranded in a foreign country with none of our belongings and had to start work the very next day! Luckily, the company's legal department and my EAP benefit helped resolve the conflict." Do your homework on the vendors to make sure there are no loose ends. Ask a lot of questions – vendors like the movers are additional resources.

Cecilia A. recalls her hectic experience in an Italian airport while studying abroad. "I lost my passport as the officials had stopped me to check it. Later on, I realized my mistake; they had kept my passport but I couldn't get back in without it. What a chance to use my budding language skills!" Later, when she was trying to get home, Cecilia encountered further difficulties. "Much to my surprise, my flight out of the country during the holidays had long since been canceled. The airline told me they had informed me months ago through my travel agent. But my travel agent had sadly passed away while I was out of the country. I know, that's tragic. Naturally, all my luggage and I were stuck in the airport until I could finally get a flight out the next day. This macabre story is almost unbelievable, but it happened to me!"

Antony R. reminisces, "I had an apartment in Florence and a home in Atlanta. It was hard keeping the bills paid for both places and keeping up with maintenance long-distance. Fortunately, I had neighbors I could call and they were lifesavers. Having someone local to keep an eye on things helped a lot."

An Ounce of Planning is Priceless

While planning in advance can't account for all the unforeseeable hiccups when traveling and relocating to a new country, the process is essential. Double-check on all travel plans ahead of time so that there is little room for communication errors.

"We rented an apartment in a Parisian suburb," said Jack K., a quality control expert. "Thinking we had planned well and worked with a relocation expert, we were confused by the two tax bills that arrived during the six month stay. The landlord turned out to be only a manager who claimed to know little English. We had no idea how to go about consulting a financial expert in Paris, especially in the suburbs, and finally we just paid the bills. It felt like extortion."

At the same time, begin tying up loose ends at home. On the big move day (or days), it is essential to have all the information available. In addition to planning the new life abroad, expatriates will need to take into consideration every part of their "old lives," from settling legal and financial accounts to saying goodbye to family and friends. Use the To-Do lists at the end of the upcoming chapters as a starting point for your own planning:

Planning and Packing To-Do's:

Make sure that visas or passports are secured well ahead of time and that there is no red tape barring entry to the country. Sometimes there are restrictions on everything from wood furniture and foods to literature and pets. Ensure pets will be allowed to remain with you during your stay. If not, it may be wise to find a relative or friend in the United States who will be willing to look after animals while away.

Create a comprehensive list of all that needs to be done. Keep it close by along with other important documents and check off items completed.

Extensively research homes, nearby conveniences and schools in the new country. Get feedback on the internet and in expatriate guides that designates the best schools and the most suitable housing for you and/or your family.

Decide how much responsibility you will maintain between home country and host country. For those on short-term assignments, it can be difficult to maintain two households.

Set aside time to pack, ship and prepare items. It will take more time than anticipated.

Never be afraid to ask for help. Friends and neighbors will be more than willing to help. The work it will take to transition from one country to another requires many hands. Utilize whatever expatriate orientations, resources and assistance your company offers.

Connect with others in the host country. This can be done ahead of time as well as upon arrival. Utilize internet resources, blogs and forums centering on the new city to meet locals and other expatriates who have shared the same journey. Their experiences can be invaluable when planning.

Money Does Make the World Go 'Round

With the ups and downs of worldwide economies, fiscal stress is affecting people to a great extent. As a result, many people may choose to escape abroad and find a more affordable way of life; especially those who have a job opportunity. Money however, is both measured and valued differently around the world.

James W., a contractor, found the differences in money and measurements to be the easy part. "You get used to it after a while, automatically converting amounts without even realizing it." The more challenging part is not planning ahead for an increase in prices and for the amount of money it will take to move. Financial failure, second only to spouses not settling in, is the next most crucial reason why expatriates return home. Those who fail to effectively plan for their relocation, who do not take into account their new cost of living in relation to their earning power abroad or who over-extend themselves with a home purchase and a fantastic lifestyle, are all at risk of financial hardship overseas. Therefore, if you're moving abroad you need to be on top of your finances before you even pick the country you're moving to. Failure to get your finances in order will hinder your chances to fulfill the expatriate dream lifestyle.

Getting a home set up abroad, buying a car, shipping furniture and finding a good school to put your children through costs money, not to mention occasional visits home as necessary. And this is just the start of money matters.

"Costa Rica was always our dream," says Brittany M. Her spouse, a highly skilled filtration expert, was assigned there to be part of a new hospital expansion project. "The rooster crowing next door seemed quaint at first. The barking dogs seemed like a safety barrier. Shopping for food daily was a delight with so many fresh choices and so much variety. My high school Spanish seemed to be working and we set out to settle in. Unfortunately, American prices had gotten there first."

"Everything seemed to cost more and was harder to get," Brittany said. "As expenses got tight, I started to have a lower tolerance for everything else. The rooster was headed for stew as far as I was concerned, the dogs were beggars and a nuisance and the romance of shopping and living abroad quickly declined when we had to shell out time and money each day for fresh food. We had both really underestimated what it would cost to live day to day in our paradise."

Once relocated, though, the real test begins. Americans used to a certain lifestyle might find accommodations and finances tight. Charles G. moved to the south of France for five months as part of a training program. He was provided with an apartment, which turned out to be too tiny for the over six-foot-tall man. He eventually learned that European accommodations tended to be smaller and more compact than in America. "The bed was tiny, smaller than a twin bed and the bedroom was so small, I couldn't even open the door all the way. Stepping over the bed was the only way to get into the bathroom. The kitchen was compact and I assumed it was a kitchenette, but found that many residents in France were used to these small spaces. For me, it felt claustrophobic." And yet larger, more spacious apartments would have cost Charles a good deal more out of his own pocket, which he learned during research. It was more financially sound to stay in the somewhat uncomfortable apartment, and, like the locals, he soon adapted.

The challenge, then, is to set a reasonable budget. When at all possible, do some research and see where and how funds are going to be allocated. The most important expenses to take into account are food, rent, insurance and transportation. It might be a good idea to research websites and contact other expatriates in the area to locate favorite grocery stores and suggestions for cutting costs on a daily basis. Avoid making large purchases right away. Go as far as skipping that deluxe cup of coffee every day. When making a major move, every penny counts. In the long run, after adjusting to life abroad with all its many unexpected challenges, there might be opportunities for a little splurge once in a while.

Make sure you are aware which expenses are being paid for by your employer, and which are your responsibility. Don't be afraid to ask questions about whether the company will cover your rental car, meals, hotels, and passport fees. Be clear on everything up front. You might assume that all your moving expenses are covered, when in reality you received a relocation allowance in a fixed amount. Get it in writing, at the least in an email. Smaller companies expanding into new markets may not have a process in place, so be sure to hammer out the details beforehand. Negotiate the details of your relocation agreement as needed. You don't want your first year abroad to put you in debt.

Sales consultant Leanne T., remembers, "I used to go to American hotels, the Hyatt or Marriott, just to eat in restaurants and pick up some toiletries in the gift shop. They were often an oasis of home in a sea of strangeness." American products are often available abroad, but can be expensive. Leanne discovered that by asking locals about less expensive day-to-day options and through careful, more realistic budgeting, she could afford to splurge every so often on familiar American items.

Though destinations like Japan and Dubai can seem outrageously expensive and some like Costa Rica cost a bit more for the same living standard, often it is a matter of education about things like currency valuation. Once relocation is complete, some expatriates can enjoy a similar paycheck while experiencing a higher quality of life. In many countries, healthcare is extremely affordable. The internet and advance planning will help with the daily business of living and working abroad.

While many Americans traveling abroad expect to maintain the same standard of living on a similar budget, they can be disappointed when they discover that not only are living essentials different in host countries, but so are the prices. It is best to be realistic about what you can spend each week on food, housing, clothing, transportation and other essentials. Planning ahead of time can help alleviate financial stress and help save for the more expensive activities, such as vacations and souvenirs, later on.

Here in the United States, the cost of living can vary widely from state to state and city to city, but variances can be even more extreme from country to country. According to Expatistan.com, the overall cost of living is 48% less in Guadalajara, Mexico than Atlanta, Georgia. On the other hand, the cost of living is 56% higher in London, England than Pittsburgh, Pennsylvania. Every dollar you earn in Guadalajara is worth $1.48, but the dollars you earn in London would only be equal to $0.44.

Research the cost of living in your destination country so you can budget accordingly. Transportation costs are 85% higher in London, but only 4% higher in Frankfurt, Germany, and 47% lower in Abu Dhabi, UAR. Reviewing the cost of living for each category of food, clothing, housing, transportation and entertainment, will allow you to easily modify your existing budget and accurately anticipate your living expenses in your new country.

Finance and Budgeting To-Do's:

Create a detailed list of expenses before leaving home, estimating how much all the essentials will cost. Whenever possible, research average prices abroad and adjust your budget accordingly.

Set a budget each week for essential items - food, rent or housing, savings, etc. Decide how much you're able to spend outside that range - but don't go over budget (very often).

Be frugal. There may be a variety of expensive start-up costs, but in the beginning of your stay, try to limit spending as much as possible until you have a better sense of what it will take, fiscally and stress-wise, to adjust to life in this new land.

Research the value of the American dollar compared to local currency. The exchange rate may be in your favor.

Managing Expectations of Life Abroad

When in anticipation of an event, people generally form expectations - about how the holiday party will go, how we will be greeted by a coworker, how we will perform in a work challenge, or where we will be in five years. Having expectations is no different in the process of relocating. Psychologically, expectations can help to build confidence and reduce anxiety in new and potentially stressful experiences. Expectations that turn out to be wildly different from reality can cause anxiety and make adapting to changes much more difficult. While individual experiences may be hard to anticipate in every instance, research will create more realistic expectations and can help stabilize the symptoms of culture shock.

An individual's sense of identity is closely tied to their sense of place, whether it is as encompassing as a common language or as seemingly simple as a trip to a favorite grocery store. Expatriates may initially feel as though they are lost or dislocated. Being friendly and open may help assuage these feelings.

Sandra G., another former expatriate, sums up her experience of feeling completely displaced. "Four years ago, I made a big decision and an even bigger move. I packed my suitcases from the cozy interior of my brand new apartment, handed over the keys of my brand new car and left my brand new job as a reporter to move to South Korea. That's right, I sacrificed my personal possessions, my current job and my social life to live in a country where I didn't know the language, didn't understand the customs and definitely didn't fit in."

Sandra may not have fit in, but she had largely anticipated the great impact the move would have on her life, and soon she had learned to adapt to her circumstances and take everything in. "I have gained more than I ever dreamed. My sacrifices were well worth it and now I am a stronger, more well-rounded and considerate individual. In the past three or four months I've struggled my share, cried in Starbucks (smells can really bring you back home), been frustrated by language barriers and disgusted by eating rituals (dog will never be my thing, nor will caterpillar larvae). But I wouldn't trade a moment of the experience. I strongly recommend that anyone who has a chance should go! My perception of the world has been stretched and changed in ways I can't describe and each experience, good or bad, has truly made me a better person."

However, when preconceived expectations are not met, the reverse may occur. As an example, during the holidays with family, when the hotel accommodations, location, food or weather exceeds expectations, we are likely to feel positive and happy. Conversely, when expectations are not met, the resulting disappointment can affect the whole mood of the holiday and attitudes towards it. A sense of humor about unmet expectations can somewhat mitigate the negative effects that unmet expectations can have.

Following are specific expectations that expatriates may encounter during their moves abroad:

Expectations regarding standards. Cleanliness, education, food and living standards are likely to be the first area of disappointment. "On a trip to Egypt, I arrived from the airport and was driving through what seemed to be the poorest part of Cairo," relates Melanie T. "I asked the English-speaking driver if this was 'downtown.' He said yes. I was shocked. I was later to learn that there was a communication breakdown. His idea of 'downtown' was definitely not the exciting and wonderful city-center of Cairo." The taxi driver's misinterpretation of her question lead to disappointment and confusion for Melanie. "My expectations were on a roller coaster. A trip to the ladies' room in a high-end hotel introduced me to the hole-and-pole system. It was something I had not expected, but quickly learned its functionality. Let's just say I would have preferred an outhouse!" Melanie's initial impressions of Cairo were that it was a dirty slum with inadequate hygiene. Eventually she was able to look past the inadequacies and learn to appreciate the culture, people and history of Egypt.

Expectations regarding agreements. Commitments made by an organization regarding support, job conditions, responsibilities, accommodations and career are all promises made at a distance. What happens upon arrival can be very different. In difficult situations, especially through language barriers, a "yes" is perceived more positively than a "no." Often this is out of politeness or a desire to please. For example, "Does the room have a view?" "Yes." The answer comes too quickly and pleases hopeful travelers, even when it may not be true. Look for internet images. Read your relocation contract carefully and ask questions.

Expectations of yourself. You might assume you will learn the language quickly, but six months later find that you continue struggle with ordering meals and understanding directions. You might assume that your winning personality will charm your colleagues and business contacts, but find that the bright, sparkling personality that helped you succeed in America is less valuable in the brusque and hurried business environment in the Middle East. Don't be afraid to ask for help, maybe a language tutor one or two nights a week. Be sure to give yourself credit for areas where your expertise and abilities are helping you exceed expectations.

Expectations of surroundings. Weather may be too hot or cold, compared to where you are from. It may be a more crowded city than you are used to, or you might find yourself in a countryside or suburban area with few conveniences. Most of the time an expat will have researched the weather or living circumstances, but lifestyle changes can be physically jolting, even if you feel mentally prepared.

Expectations of lifestyle. If you are used to making a stop at your local Starbucks every morning, and find there are NO Starbucks in your city (heaven forbid), it can change your quality of life. You may have expected to find a home like the ones you see on *House Hunters International*, and be disappointed in the "quaint" (translate to "broken down") places available. You may expect to find new friends waiting for you at the local pub, only to find the locals unfriendly to new faces.

Expectations are really a form of hope. Hope for a spacious house or a cliff-side villa with a pool; hope that your language skills are better than they are; hope for plenty of travel opportunities and so on. Keep the hope, let go of assumptions, confirm on your own or via a trusted resource.

When Elsa M. traveled to India, she was given several bowls after dinner at a restaurant. One was a bowl of water, one was filled with something that looked like sand, and one held a pale powder. Confused, she assumed that they had ritual purpose, as she had expected that everything about Indian culture was infused with religious significance. She was surprised to find out the bowls were for very practical purposes. One was for washing her hands, and the last was a sort of after-dinner mint. Her expectations had been disproved, luckily this time for the better. As in many cases, the reality of foreign culture is full of surprises.

How does one resolve the issue of unmet expectations? Spend time learning about the culture in your destination. Consider how you will need to think and behave to operate effectively. Be open-minded and resourceful. Remember that planning can only go so far. To be truly successful as an expatriate, one must be willing to quickly change plans or problem-solve if something goes awry. The corporate Employee Assistance Program (EAP) or relocation vendor can be a significant source of help and resources. Check out these programs before leaving.

Research Tip

Have each member of your family research one aspect of life in your new country (money, travel, local dress and customs, traditional foods) and present this information to the group. Allow each person to **become the family expert in one area**.

Goal Setting: Get SMART and START

What constitutes expatriate success? Completing the year or two of your planned stay? Learning the local language? Deciding to stay permanently? Each individual and family group will have their own goals in regards to their upcoming stay in another country. The employee moving may do so to advance their career. A trailing spouse may want to explore the world. Parents may want their children to have a larger perspective on life in the world. Your daughter may want to make connections for studying abroad in college. Your son may want to go to a soccer game and watch a famous player. Your family may want to see the Pyramids of Giza, the Eiffel Tower, the Taj Mahal, ski the Swiss alps, or eat pizza in Italy.

It is important to understand, both from an individual and a family perspective, what you want to get out of your trip abroad. Write down your goals, and have each of your family members to do the same. Sit down as a group and brainstorm things you want to do during your stay abroad. It's a great way to get everyone excited about going on your trip.

A mission statement might also be helpful, and can even be displayed on the refrigerator to remind the family on a daily basis what their goals are.

The Jones Family Mission Statement for their two-year assignment in England:

The Jones Family is spending two years in England so that they may take advantage of the opportunity to live abroad, travel Europe, see the sights, and learn about other cultures.

Here are some goals that might help you and your family get started:

- Become fluent in a second language
- Explore a city
- See famous monuments, statues, buildings, bridges (be specific)
- Go to museums, see famous works of art (be specific)
- Go to sporting events, theater productions
- Make contacts for future trips abroad
- Career advancement
- Make friends
- Missionary or volunteer work
- Living abroad for college application
- Vacations on the beach, at ski resorts, or in famous cities (be specific)

Goals should be SMART: Specific, Measurable, Achievable, Relevant, and Timely. "Learn French" is a fairly vague and broad goal. "Order a meal in French" or "Speak French for an entire day" are more specific, measurable and achievable. Once specific goals are achieved, new and more advanced goals can be established. Rewards can be created for achieving more challenging goals, like a trip to a sporting event or museum, dinner at a special restaurant, or a weekend getaway.

Goals should be reviewed periodically and adjusted, using START: Set a goal, Try it out, Assess your success, Rework and reframe, and Try, try again. This practice will be addressed in more detail in Stage 5.

Involving the entire family in the planning process allows everyone to have a voice, to provide their affirmation, and establishes a vision for a successful expatriate experience. Make sure to review your list of Expatriate Goals after a few months, to ensure you make the time to do the things you hoped to do at the outset of your trip, and not lose sight of the reasons you agreed to make the trip. Success is important for every individual in the group.

Goal Planning Tip

Establish some **key goals for both career and leisure.** This will encourage you to move forward with balance, dedicating time to both work and relaxation.

Coping Strategies: Keep Calm and Carry On

Success may not come without challenges. Like playing a golf course, you hope to avoid the traps and hazards, but inevitably you will find yourself in the sand or the trees. The best players know that a good recovery shot can put you right back on track. There has likely never been a trip abroad that has not encountered some level of difficulty. Be prepared for the glitches, lost items, missing forms, long lines and difficult people. Remember to pat yourself on the back when you get through each unexpected challenge with grace and dignity. Treat people respectfully and refrain from expressing anger and frustration. A smile is understood in any language. "Can you help me?" is often the best way to solicit assistance.

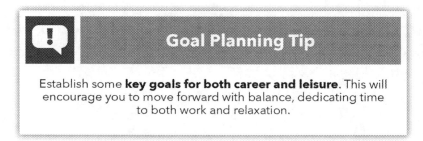

Difficulties during the first weeks of relocation can cause frustration and discouragement for the expatriate. Often, help can come in the form of HR professionals or professional third-party services, such as relocation experts or Employee Assistance Programs (EAP's). Training programs can be very effective in facilitating expatriate adjustment to the conditions and culture of the host country. If an organization offers pre-assignment orientation, take advantage of all such educational opportunities. Topics such as intercultural communication and business strategies, managing expectations and stress, and building meaningful work relationships are essential parts of the orientation process and preparation needed once expatriates reach the destination country.

"I remember my HR department had me view a training video for expatriates," says Adrian E, who moved to Japan over a year ago. "I couldn't believe how complex all the little rules were for greeting business partners, communicating with them and delivering presentations. I thought I would never remember it all! But once I got there and met my first contact in Japan, it all came back to me. I would have definitely made a fool of myself without that training."

Third-party relocation specialists can provide host country representatives to help orient expatriates. If at all possible, work with others at your destination office who have been through the expatriation process. Locals can be a great help. Interaction with host country nationals and expatriates can provide essential tips and encouragement. Meeting local residents and socializing can serve as a great bridge, and encourage the expatriate to model local behavior, making the transition to the host country smoother and more seamless. Such contacts can be found through a third-party professional, the company office, or by becoming part of an international community online. This preparation is important in the early days of the assignment when stress is high and settling in is most chaotic.

"For me, success was when I realized we had stayed an extra year longer than the original assignment," says Andrew S., an English teacher in Korea. "Living abroad became not just a temporary trip but a way of life. At that point, Indiana was a part of my past and Korea was my future. I realized I was happy in both cultures."

However well-matched a candidate and assignment are and no matter the amount of planning, complications are bound to arise, whether related to technicalities such as entering the country, work-related, cultural stress, or personal stressors. When such issues occur for the individual, it is important to remember that the expatriate is not the only one heavily invested in this endeavor. Corporations can assist, either directly or through third-party professionals, in ensuring that the relocation is a success. It never hurts to ask what resources are available.

Red Tape Tip

Be patient! There will be delays with bank accounts, visas, work permits, leases, and other bureaucracy. **Be prepared for snags along the way.** Look for the lesson. "That was challenging, but I learned how to navigate customs, did not lose my temper, and found a helpful person." Don't be afraid to reach out to your employer, HR, EAP or consulate for help.

Two types of coping skills employed by expatriates when facing difficult hurdles are: **symptom-focused** and **problem-focused**. The approaches in symptom-focused strategies are used to diminish emotional distress by attending to behavior and expression, physiological disturbance, and subjective distress. While temporarily useful, symptom-focused coping strategies do not eliminate the issue, leaving room for concerns to grow and fester.

Problem-focused coping strategies are efforts to take constructive action to change the situation creating the stress, address the problem directly and minimize the anxiety and distress. Expatriates who use the problem-focused coping strategy may be able to better cope with the stress. However, the symptom-focused coping strategy may help in defining the problem. Good coping skills are critical for expatriates to overcome relocation challenges.

Confusion with foreign money caused frustration for Debbie J. during her first days in Italy. Whenever she and her husband were together, she asked him to take charge of paying for things, a symptom-based strategy which relieved her immediate discomfort, but did not resolve the issue. After speaking with her local HR contact about her difficulties with handling money, she was given a "cheat sheet" to use, which greatly simplified the process of paying for items, and gave her confidence going forward, to the point where she became the expert, and started paying for items on her husband's behalf. This problem-focused strategy addressed the issue, rather than side-stepping it.

Ultimately, much of the work in assimilating to the new culture is a matter of acceptance. But, by taking steps to ensure an organization offers support throughout the process, expats can start off on the right foot. Companies can provide a framework of support that an employee can easily access in stressful times. Make sure you are acquainted with the resources.

The Three R's for Stage 1: Preparation:

Recognize that what you expect and hope for as you move abroad will very likely change drastically. Recognize the need to be flexible and re-evaluate. Research and resources will help in adapting and reducing difficulty. Nothing will be totally predictable. Being able to relax and even laugh a little in the face of adversity will pay great dividends when things inevitably do take a slight deviation from the grand plan.

Respond by determining whether expectations are based on what you know to be true or what you hope to be true. If it is a question of what you hope to be true, then set about researching the reality surrounding your hopes and adjust them where necessary. List your expectations for standards and of that list, choose a few that are the most important to you. As far as agreements go, triple-check to ensure that each party is clear about what is to be expected. Make it a principle to deal in agreements rather than verbal contracts. For example, "We agreed that you would have a short list of properties for viewing by today."

Reinforce by managing your expectations, even when everything seems to go askew. Set short-term goals for "must-dos," even if it is as simple as going to the market once a week or visiting with family via webcam on a set date. If unmet expectations are overwhelming, these few routine accomplishments can make everything seem a little bit more manageable. Reinforce even the small successes by rewarding yourselves when your goals are met. People under stress need extra pats on the back.

Stage 2: Transition

"When you travel, remember that a foreign country is not designed to make you comfortable. It is designed to make its own people comfortable."
– Clifton Fadiman

The transition from the home country to host country can produce what sometimes seems like an intolerable amount of stress. In almost all cases, the responsibilities of expatriates in emerging countries will be larger than they are used to overseeing, in their work environments, personal lives and integration with a new culture.

Given the nature of emerging countries in Southeast Asia, managerial expatriates may supervise five to ten times more people than is average. To illustrate, a German IT Manager who managed 15 people in his home country could have 100 people to manage in Malaysia. An American Call Center Manager with 100 people in the U.S. can find himself soon overseeing 800 in the Philippines. Such large increases in responsibility are difficult for anyone to handle, especially for an expatriate. In addition to that are the new challenges of managing expectations of head office managers and clients in other countries who may not understand the cultural differences that are impacting results.

It is important that both the organizations and the expatriates be able to manage stress for organizational and individual well-being. Both host nationals and employees within the host country employ different coping strategies depending on effectiveness across various regions. Expatriates can be active participants in individual adjustment processes, especially with emphasis on strong problem-solving skills, a willingness to change, and high performance, among other factors. These characteristics will help ensure successful adjustment, even though employees of all personality types may be fully capable of handling any shift in responsibilities and considerations that may arise.

The transition can be jarring at first. Feeling overwhelmed while juggling multiple responsibilities, new laws, new regulations and expatriate stress is inevitable. Managing these obligations will be crucial in the success of the assignment. But, with careful consideration of the many tasks an expatriate must consider when moving abroad, foreign assignment success is a perfectly reasonable goal.

Career Advancement: The Stairway to New Opportunities

Working abroad can provide unique life and career experiences, and can enhance employment and promotional opportunities. It can help sharpen diversity and communication skills that are already in place. For those who enjoy travel, a job opportunity in another country allows the expatriate easier access to other areas of the world. Micah L. writes, "Moving to Rome was the best decision I ever made. Traveling throughout Europe is not only easy, but cheap, if you do the right research. It was perfect for a nomad like me. Prior to pursuing a master's in Architectural History, I traveled within my budget. I easily flew from Rome to Paris, trained on the EuroStar from Paris to London, took the Stena Line Super Ferry from Harwich to Holland and trained on the EuroStar from Amsterdam to Paris all for around six hundred dollars. Oh and don't even ask me where I slept! Between bed and breakfasts, hostels (absolutely do your research before staying!) and sleeping on the trains, the bed expense was pretty cheap, which allowed me to splurge here and there."

Whether the job experience or life experience or both are attractive, working abroad can be a huge stepping stone. Living abroad can provide a broader range of job options and the opportunity to change careers. Setting clear goals for career advancement will increase chances of success. Erin P. says, “When I decided to pursue a different career path, I knew I would need to gain experience in my new field. I figured that if I was going to quit my job and start over again, I might as well gain that experience somewhere new and exciting. I did my research and found a program that gave me the opportunity to intern at a well-known company in my desired field abroad. Not only did I gain valuable job experience for my resume, I got to travel, learn a new language, and immerse myself in a different culture and lifestyle. It was an incredible experience, and when I returned home, I was able to begin working right away due to my newly-acquired skills and knowledge.”

Taking on heavy responsibilities as an expatriate can be a perk in itself. It looks great on a resume. Moving and working abroad shows cultural cognizance, problem-solving skills and the flexibility to change, all qualities that can dramatically increase career value and appeal to employers.

Erika F., a scientist with the Army Corps of Engineers who worked in Iraq for six months says, “It was so interesting seeing another part of the world, especially one which had so much conflict. All my friends were really impressed I would voluntarily go over there, especially when it was a little scary! Honestly, the scariest part was adjusting to an entirely different work environment and changing my managing style. When I got back to Oregon, my boss promptly offered me a raise. Even though it was hard at first, I kind of enjoyed working abroad and I didn’t know why he had suddenly become so generous! In retrospect, it was definitely worth it, both personally and professionally.”

Similarly, even a failed posting can boost credibility, but with less certainty. Sometimes, a failed posting can even damage a candidate’s career, considering it costs a company upwards of tens of thousands of dollars to send the expatriate abroad (not exactly a winning recommendation). That is why careful planning is essential in ensuring expatriate success.

Learning about a foreign country and its customs will lend specific expertise that will help boost a company's accessibility, profits and reliability in both domestic and foreign markets. Put that knowledge to good use by adapting individual managerial styles to the environment. Senior Vice President of International Relations, Paulina S., says, "When I moved back home, everyone at my company came to me with questions, not just about how my experience was, but about how people in Dubai would respond to different situations, products or materials we were going to send them. I usually knew the answers. Plus, I had friends there who I could always ask or call in favors from. It was the best of both worlds!"

Sinola S. was a 40-year-old lawyer living in Wyoming when she decided to make the move abroad. It was a result of several jobs she'd obtained in Peru and Chile. "I just thought- why not live there, since I'm already working there anyway?" As she began going back and forth between clients in the U.S. and clients abroad, Sinola began to morph into a lawyer who could do more than one thing. "I found myself expanding my passions to include criminal law, anti-corruption and legal reform. It's wonderful and I've never looked back." She had first-hand experience in international law and quickly became an expert in it and as a result, her small firm quickly grew to include all types of international legal business.

Working abroad looks great on a resume, boosts hireability and can create specialty expertise if taken advantage of. Simply going overseas is not proof of the qualities and expertise desired for an international worker. What really makes one stand out from the crowd is flexibility and creative managing. Kain M., who worked in India for two years, says, "When I was in the States, I thought I had everything figured out to fix the profitability crisis my company was having. Just fire this guy, hire some new people in this area and be more aggressive with marketing. When I actually showed up in

India, it turned out to be a whole different story. I had to change the way I'd planned to do things from a cultural perspective and from a business perspective to get the job done. No firing! A real challenge!"

Career Advancement To-Do's:

Make a list of concrete career and business goals to be achieved when working abroad. Keep these goals small and flexible as a sense of the situation evolves. When this inevitably occurs, modify goals.

If you're not sure what moving abroad might do to benefit your future, ask.

An overseas posting can help with goal achievement. What steps can be taken to make the most of being an expatriate? (Learn a new language? Make some foreign friends? Explore a new culture? Branch out to international business groups? Reorganize an office space?)

Work Assimilation: Taking Your Job Abroad

Transitioning to a new workforce, even in the same job role, often presents problems of assimilation. Host country coworkers may be resistant to taking orders from a foreign manager, and responsibilities of the job may expand to include more demanding obligations. The key to integrating with a new workforce is to be persistent and stick with the process. Letting coworkers know that the goal is to work on a plan of self-integration may ease their perceptions of being threatened or harboring prejudices. Empower coworkers as agents for change. Enlist local support and suggestions and maintain openness when new challenges arise.

John O., an architecture manager in Japan, struggled to connect with his coworkers at first. "I couldn't understand it," he says. "They were always slipping me these dirty glares and purposefully avoiding communicating with me directly. I was at my wit's end, until this cab driver refused to take my money and carefully explained to me that I was giving him money with my 'dirty' hand. My coworkers had thought that I was purposefully insulting them by handing them dirty papers! No wonder they'd avoided me. Once I explained it to them, they laughed. Overall, it was a real learning experience for all of us."

Motivation is the key to persistence. Motivation itself is not a goal. Motivation is a byproduct of desire. Daily goal review helps. Those goals range from meeting corporate goals to achieving personal success, which includes excelling in the placement and meeting SMART goals – specific, measurable, achievable, realistic and timely.

Dealing with the stress of the workload, coworkers and workplace attitudes will take some experience. But change and adaptation are inevitable. Despite obvious cultural differences, adapting to a new work environment in another country is much the same as adapting to a new work environment in the U.S. Remember that awkward first day, when you weren't sure whether to laugh or nod along seriously with the inside jokes that flew around? Each company, near or far, has a different atmosphere. Patience in learning to accept and adapt will go a long way in transitioning to the new work situation.

Take Amanda T., for instance, who moved to France to work in a biochemistry lab. While she normally thrived in social situations, it seemed like her coworkers went out of their way to avoid being friendly to her. "One day I sat down with them at the cafeteria and wished them a good afternoon, commenting on something that had happened earlier in the lab. They all looked at each other and started laughing, even my manager! I was so humiliated; I didn't talk to them again for weeks. But then one day I got in a really bad accident and what do you know - I was surprised to see them walk in the hospital door with flowers and get-well cards. 'What happened?' I asked them. 'I thought you all hated me.' My manager said that they were just getting back at me for my lousy French. I've since learned to accept their humor - I used to be so sensitive! Thank goodness I finally asked them what I had done to offend them. Turned out,

I hadn't done much of anything. They were just joking around as they usually do!"

Making an effort to learn the customs and culture of coworkers can definitely ease the strain of transition. Be receptive to trying new things and accepting feedback, whether it is negative or positive. It will serve as a good learning experience nonetheless. Coworkers will appreciate being listened to. Some might even be overly enthusiastic about giving feedback and knowing their opinions are valued. Being open to change is essential, considering the expat has come into a pre-established environment. But remember that bridge goes both ways. After listening to coworkers, engage in the conversation by adding something like, "I understand that I'm not being clear. I will work harder to make the assignment clearer next time. But where I come from, this language means to do it in this certain way." Understanding will help both parties communicate expectations better in the long run.

Joe M. says, "I was having dinner with a group of managers in my corporate rental. At the last minute, I remembered I knew nothing about the drinking customs of my peers who lived in this primarily Muslim country. We quickly whisked the wine glasses off the table and my wife began making lemonade. We weren't even sure about coffee or tea!"

A good way to ease into the work environment is through small talk. The typical "water-cooler" conversation can help with understanding coworkers on a more personal level and building relationships. However, what might be a perfectly reasonable question in one culture, such as, "How are your kids?" might be far too invasive in another. You may also find yourself on the awkward side of the conversation. Arielle H., a Canadian working in Singapore, experienced this within the first few days of her new job. "I thought I'd stay safe with the Canadian custom of asking about my coworker's weekend and chatting about the weather. I was shocked to hear her reply with questions about how much money I made, how much money my husband made, how much I paid for my apartment and how often I went shopping. I stumbled out some evasive reply, too startled to even think about how I should answer."

Arielle reflected later about how she handled the situation and how she could have done better. "I knew that in Singapore, there was no shame in questions about money. The woman was just trying to figure out where my station was relative to hers. To her, it was a perfectly natural thing to ask. I should have realized then what it really was to be an expatriate, not only to assimilate with the strange culture quirks, but to be able to switch back and forth between fundamentally different ways of thinking. It would have been an even better learning experience for both of us if I'd said something like, 'We Canadians don't really talk about money, eh?'" Though she still does not expect herself to do everything perfectly, Arielle viewed the learning experience as a pathway to deeper understanding of Singapore's culture and values. She was able to connect with Beth after a few more cultural stumbles and make a good work friend, a relationship which helped deepen her connection to the host country.

Relationships might not be the only challenge encountered in the new workplace. Increasing demands on time and energy will tax many expatriates' stamina. Different computer systems and technological constraints (or lack thereof) on the other side of the world may inhibit productivity. Workloads will seem especially difficult along with the inevitable stresses of culture shock and settling in to a new location, added to the fact that expatriates will likely be dealing with more work and managing more employees than ever before. Be sure to make use of any support system or EAP's that are available. Beyond that, the best advice would be to challenge, motivate and reward after accomplishing productivity goals.

Work Adjustment Tip

If you find yourself comparing your new country's office with your home country, stop yourself. Comments like "In America, we used to handle project reports this way," can create animosity and label you as a complainer. Instead **try using complimentary statements** like "This is an interesting approach to project reports, I may have to show them your methods when I return to America."

Be patient when learning new information. Take advantage of the experiences of those expats who have gone before you. Time may be short to learn the cultural ins and outs of good business practices, but by working piece by piece, a little bit at a time, assimilation can be functional as well as successful.

Work Assimilation To-Dos:

Make an effort to meet and interact with new coworkers, using research to learn local mores.

If you make a cultural faux pas, say something like, "I'm sorry, I didn't know what that meant," or "In my home country, we do this differently. I am still learning the customs here." Use it as an opportunity to clarify intent and build understanding.

Stay consistently motivated to learn from mistakes.

Be open and available, both as a manager and as an employee. It will create a more accessible environment for people to keep the lines of communications open.

When in doubt, ask questions; many of them.

Smile and learn to laugh at yourself. Being offended will only put up walls where you want to build bridges.

Maintaining Your Good Health

Encouraging healthy life habits might actually be easier in foreign cultures that are very family-oriented. Video game culture is often less prominent outside of the United States, and more time spent with family usually means less time in front of the television or the computer screen. You may notice families abroad are likely to be more physically active. Fast foods, while growing in popularity, are also less ubiquitous outside of the U.S. Convenience food products may be few and far between. This of course means that one will need to learn to prepare meals with the foods that are available. This cultural adjustment can be a fun culinary adventure for some, but others will find the lack of favorite comfort foods a difficult hurdle to overcome.

HALT Tip

You might find that everything is harder to do abroad. Grocery shopping, driving from one place to another, paying bills. HALT can add to your frustration with daily tasks. Don't get **Hungry**, **Angry**, **Lonely** or **Tired**, and you'll find that things get easier. Stop to eat, rest or call someone, and you'll find a new perspective.

Arlene T., an expatriate spouse, says "In the first month of being in Cairo, I realized there were no bars. There was no BevMo! down the street or drunks on street corners. I realized how pleasant it was visiting tourist attractions with busy coffee bars instead of alcohol. The whole atmosphere seemed...well, I don't know...just more peaceful. It was certainly a positive experience."

Physical activity in other countries is often not a matter of scheduling a walk once a week; it can become part of the daily routine. Walking to work or to the supermarket is normal and in certain locations, transportation is physically demanding in itself. Changon T. writes, "I couldn't believe how organized and detailed all the biking routes were in the Netherlands. They had a numbered system to track biking distances and route, even in unfamiliar cities - and here, *everyone* rides a bike everywhere."

In spite of the most extreme precautions, illness will occur. Prepare by bringing a stash of "tummy"-related over-the-counter drugs and remedies. They may not be readily at hand in your new country when vomiting and diarrhea, regardless of the cause, occurs. Also, pharmacies are not as plentiful, nor English-speaking doctors. Expatriates may inevitably experience food or water related illnesses shortly after moving. Leah B. says, "When I moved to Israel, my roommates and I were having horrible stomach problems during our first few weeks there. We finally realized that we weren't used to eating so much yogurt, cottage cheese and hummus – staples in the Israeli diet – and we had to back off the dairy products until our bodies could adjust to the new foods."

Though most countries have a water regulation system and are very good about providing clean drinking water, others are more uncertain. Bottled water is the safest. When in doubt, boil water before drinking to kill any bacterium that might reside there. As for avoiding illnesses, general health conditions vary enormously throughout the world and expatriates will need to educate themselves about these conditions so that the proper immunizations or other precautions can be taken and cleanliness standards upheld. Medical practices also vary widely, including pregnancy care, vaccination programs for infants and young children and emergency care, just to name a few. Hand washing will help prevent contracting illnesses.

Laura M. had a pleasantly surprising experience while visiting her husband's family for the first time in Pakistan. "I'm giving my three-year-old daughter a bath as usual and like every parent horror story begins, I turned my head for one second when she slips and falls. I pick her up, but she starts crying and saying, 'My arm, my arm.' One quick glance at that little arm and I'm convinced it's broken. So I scoop up my daughter, swollen arm and all and tell my husband, 'We need to get her an X-ray right now.'

Laura continues, "In America, I would probably just go to the emergency room, get the insurance cards out and probably wait for 12 hours before seeing the doctor. To my surprise, things were much better in Pakistan. First, we pull up to this radiology place in the middle of a strip mall (for lack of a better term). As soon as we walk in, we are immediately ushered back into the X-ray room. In less than one minute, my daughter gets her X-rays taken and the doctor reviews the scans. Nothing's broken (thank goodness!). Five minutes and ten dollars later, we are on our way. I must say, this was a surprisingly effortless experience."

Laura's story gives hope to those worried about medical emergencies in a foreign country. Though it's not too hard to find hospital horror stories abroad (not to mention in our own country!), there are sometimes urgent care facilities and doctors whose expertise is specific to expatriates. It can be comforting to know there may be resources available. Check for both English-speaking pharmacies and medical care ahead of time if possible.

Bella T. went to work and study in Paris. She and her parents made sure to check on her medical insurance ahead of time and were assured they had the right numbers for international coverage and that any emergency room would take her. When she unexpectedly became seriously ill with a kidney infection, she and a fellow student went to the nearest combination drug store and small hospital where drugs are dispensed, but she received the wrong drug. After conducting a little internet research, they eventually found an American hospital. She was placed in-patient until the worst had passed, was given IV medication and liquids to increase hydration. Her parents spoke with her friend and told him this was probably the only invitation that he would ever get asking him to spend the night with their daughter. He did and they were reassured. The next morning all was well, and as a bonus from the French healthcare system, she was told that there would be no charge for services.

Even the most thoroughly prepared expatriates can't plan for every contingency. A translator in Germany found that her experience at the doctor's office with what she thought was a broken foot lasted only three hours instead of three weeks, as she had expected. An English teacher in Korea actually moved there primarily for the low healthcare costs and was delighted when she spent only the equivalent of fifty American dollars at the emergency room, covering every service and medication she was provided. Ultimately it all depends on the location and the local doctors. For some, it might be a hassle and a nightmare to visit the emergency ward in a foreign country, especially where doctors don't necessarily speak English. But, for many, despite the inevitable worry, they encounter efficiency and top quality care.

The suggestions below may help make staying healthy easier:

Health To-Dos:

In your research, include information about local hospitals where English is spoken, pricing and how convenient it is to access them.

Make health a priority. If the locals have a great healthy fish dish they love to serve, try making it yourself. If they ride bikes everywhere, invest in one and use it for local transportation instead of a car. If they drink tea socially instead of alcohol, join them. Not only will your body feel better, but it can be a great way to adjust to the culture and make new friends.

Stock up on any prescription medications or over-the-counter drugs needed.

Stay fit in mind and body. The expatriate workload can take a toll physically as well as mentally and can wear on the immune system. Take opportunities to rest and take vitamins.

The Three R's for Stage 2: Transition:

Recognize just how much energy planning and transitioning will take. If overwhelmed at first, take stock of physical signs and emotions and then work to get healthier. Realize that fatigue is perfectly normal and usually wears off after time and experience with the nuances of foreign law, health, finance and work.

Respond by finding communities and resources dedicated to helping expatriates adjust. Be sociable and build local contacts and friendships that will provide support through the inevitable life challenges, offering practical advice for questions.

Reinforce by planning ahead, putting newfound knowledge into action and being proactive in making the stay in the host country as successful as possible. In the first few months abroad, tackle challenges that encourage success, such as biking a few blocks to the grocery store or simply learning everyone's names in the office. Continue to challenge yourself step by step. The more self-satisfaction achieved, the greater the chance of exceeding expectations in the assignment.

Stage 3: Settling In

"At the beginning we learn to travel,
then we travel to learn."
- William Least Heat-Moon

While the excitement of your new environment may seem like a vacation at the beginning, that "romance" may soon give way to frustration and resentment when expectations are not met and the stresses of day-to-day life pile on. Without the old local comforts that Americans were used to, such as a favorite grocery store, fitness club or even a regular routine, life abroad can seem lonely and displaced. A sense of identity is strongly tied to a sense of place and so, without the old place, partners may have to completely re-imagine or even re-invent who they are.

Eventually the transition phase of moving to a new country gives way to settling in and finding one's place in their new world. A daily routine develops, and true to Maslow's hierarchy of needs, once the basics of food, shelter and safety are fulfilled, then human beings are freed to move up to satisfying the more esoteric needs of love, belonging, esteem and self-actualization. Once expatriates are able to negotiate buying groceries, paying bills, using trains, buses or driving city streets, and mastering enough language to get by, then they are able to begin expanding their efforts to meeting friends, socializing with coworkers, going out to films or theater, and joining groups. Keep in mind that for all the members of the expatriate family, there needs to be a certain level of confidence in handling basic needs in the new country before they can graduate to wanting more out of their life. Keeping the hierarchy in mind may help manage expectations and timelines.

Family Matters

Whether it is that faithful mutt from the local animal rescue or the extended family members that crowd your home during holidays, everyone has a family. Some corporate postings are for the individual only, while others are for the immediate family to be relocated. In either situation, there is a balance that needs to be righted in the family.

While young children may be more adaptive to change, they may also display confusion and lack of social grace during the move abroad. Who looks after the kids during the day? How do you help them understand cultural differences? How are they getting to school? *Where* are they going to school?

And what about those friends that are family? Leaving everyone at home while you experience adventures abroad can be overwhelming. Their lives go on and so do yours, just in different directions. Lack of easy access to the same support groups as before may send expatriates out looking for new friends and new means of communication. New possibilities for connections and relationships begin. But, between cultural and language barriers and the strain of limited time, expatriates often find themselves longing for friends at home.

Daily Routine Tip

Make a written plan that you can follow every day. Keep it reasonable, but **push yourself to do something beyond just the basics** of work, meals, and school. Venture out physically and emotionally beyond your comfort zone. Your energies will pay dividends toward a fulfilling life.

With expatriate families experiencing so many swift changes happening all at once, it's easy to feel overwhelmed. Luckily, there is good news: Loneliness and changing familial roles need not impede the expatriate experience. They are opportunities for stronger connections within the family, growth and learning about each other and the world around us, and of course, new friends.

The Trailing Spouse

The trailing spouse, the partner that accompanies the worker who received the foreign assignment, can face an equal or even greater challenge than their partners. Few can rely on the working spouse to be an active partner in the early part of adjustment in a foreign country. As a result, the spouses of expatriates spend a lot of time by themselves. And yes, trailing spouses are still usually female.

Expatriate workers - whether managers, executives, models or technicians - are usually challenged and excited about their new postings. They may spend more time than usual at work since they are under pressure to adapt to the new culture. Frequently, the overall weight of their responsibilities is often larger than those experienced in the U.S.

At the same time, the spouse is regularly dealing with problems for which she has no previous experience. She may catch a maid stealing or be harassed by locals on the street. Liz W., has traveled widely with her husband, a principal in American schools abroad. She describes her "surrender" in American-friendly Turkey. "Each time I would go into the market place (which is almost daily there, where diets consist mainly of fresh food) I was jeered at, harassed and ridiculed by men and sometimes women. Don't get me wrong. It was only a handful each time. But it just wore me down. So I decided to give in and wore a hijab when I went shopping. The upside was I could wear my sweats or ratty jeans under the robe. That was some compensation!"

It will come as no surprise to know that it may be the spouse who faces the greatest culture challenges in this new environment. Unlike the relocated or working spouse, trailing spouses may not have been given special training from the organization and must deal more directly with cultural incongruities without understanding locals at work. Shifting roles and responsibilities on both spouses all at once can be strenuous on the marriage. The result can be an unhappy partner whose challenges overwhelm and may inadvertently begin to impact the performance of the expatriate worker. Unofficial numbers from the Asian Development Bank, a large organization modeled after the World Bank, indicate that upwards of 50 percent of their expatriates' marriages fail due to the stress of offshore postings. The consequence is that many expatriate postings are either terminated early or the performance of the expatriate employee is impaired, resulting in their termination. Once again, human and corporate capital is lost. Dr. Neill Carson,[7] developer of the International Assignment Profile, recommends a comprehensive assessment of the strengths and weaknesses of each individual involved in the posting to better prepare partners for the challenges they may face and gauge the readiness of going overseas together.

The role as head of the household presents a unique set of obstacles for expatriate women, as well as those men who play the Mr. Mom role. The work of caring for children, food, shopping and keeping the household in sync are undervalued enough. But when the stress of culture shock and language barriers are thrown in, ordinary stress can grow to epic proportions. No wonder surveys show that expatriate women find it more difficult to adjust to a foreign culture than men.

Being the trailing spouse is far more difficult than it sounds. Often, this person is leaving behind a job or career to accompany

---

7 Dr. Neill Carson with the Levinson Leadership Institute is an expert in competitive organizational structures. A former fellow at Yale, Dr. Carson received his doctorate as well as an MBA from the University of Houston.

the spouse abroad. Spouses must contend with a foreign language, familiarize themselves with unknown surroundings, find where and how to do the shopping, adjust to different daily rhythms and monetary systems, deal with children and schools and quite often they are on their own, without much of a support system. In time, friends will be made, connections will be formed, and memories will be created. But in the moment, it can be very discouraging[8].

Coping Tip

Having a rough day in your new life abroad? Things not going well? Take a quick written inventory of things you have done right, accomplishments since you arrived, progress you have made. Everyone needs a pat on the back now and then, so be sure to **compliment yourself on what you've done right** (and your family when needed). This will give you a boost through the trials that are bound to come. Review the list with your spouse or family member, so they can share your successes.

It is not uncommon for the spouse and children to feel lost, alone, overcome by culture shock, and under-appreciated. Studies show that spousal adjustment to a new location is one of the most important factors in helping overseas employees to acclimate.[9] The challenges that trailing spouses face are very real and, in fact, 65 percent of employee-sponsored expatriates who failed to complete their assignments cite a dissatisfied spouse as the primary reason.

The spouse may have been expecting to find some suitable employment, like being an English teacher, but whether for financial, career or other objectives, the spouse may have a difficult time finding work in a new country. Maggie P. tells about a very real problem for the accompanying spouse or partner. "Apart from the

---

8 Butler, "Challenges."

9 Brown, "Dominant stressors."

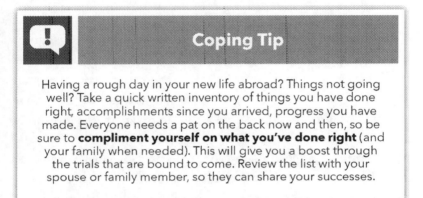

fact that we had to learn how to light fires and sweep chimneys (I was sure nobody had done this in England since Victorian times), the rock in my shoe was our job situation. Michael had his posting work, but nobody seemed to want me. What could I do besides hiring myself out as a chimney sweep? My new enthusiasm for gardening seemed unlikely to pay dividends either. For some reason there didn't seem to be a market for tons of organically grown radishes, not in this corner of County Down. Take it from one who knows - do not sow four packets of radish seeds all at once." The inability to find employment is not only damaging to the self-esteem and to the resume, but puts a deficit in the family financial picture.

While most trailing spouses are still mostly female, the trend is changing. About 20 percent of expatriate assignees in 2012 were women[10]. Male trailing spouses face the same challenges as any other (including isolation, difficulty finding a job, managing a household and looking after the kids), but in many cases, they have the added complication of dealing with traditional gender roles that are still prevalent in many other cultures around the world. They may face a lack of any type of cultural support system and even, in some cases, downright ridicule for their new roles. The transition is especially difficult for men who have given up careers in order to follow the spouse. Brian P. recalls, "It was weird, the looks the guys give you. They ask you how much money you make and you just don't know how to answer."

The internal struggle to make meaning out of one's life overseas is something that spouses of all genders will have to contend with. The external struggle is one that will vary, of course, by region. Though many cultures are still entrenched in gender role stereotyping, others may be even more accepting than American culture. "I had very little trouble," Jerome B. says. "All the moms accepted me right away, making jokes at how much of a change it must be for me, and men who had jobs just sort of commiserated and offered help.

---

10 "Global Relocation," 10.

Expatriating is hard on everyone at first, I guess. But the best part was just spending more time with my kids, which I'd always wanted but never had time for before this opportunity came along."

Fortunately, there is a growing awareness of these spousal issues that have not been given much attention in the past. Businesses that are becoming more aware of how their consideration of family needs will improve worker productivity are moving toward offering more support to trailing spouses. They are also working to encourage better preparation in language skills and cultural understanding before relocation and building stronger support networks for family members at their overseas locations.

The choice to move should really be made by both you and your significant other. If your partner is reluctant to move, have an open conversation with him or her in order to understand what the reservations are. Alternately, if you are the one who is reluctant, question your reasons why. Are you close to your family? Though you may be moving far away, it is relatively simple to stay in touch with family members through email, live video chat, phone and other services that connect loved ones across great distances. Are you simply nervous about starting a new life in a new location? Consider the adventure that few people will have in their lives. It may take time, but you will make new friends and make new and exciting discoveries.

Similarly, take some time to consider the new roles each spouse will assume. Does the trailing spouse plan to find work? If so, start looking, the sooner the better. Reach out through the working spouse's organization to see if there are resources for job searches. Who will take care of the children? Who will do most of the shopping and planning? Who will take care of the bills? Start discussions early so you're not surprised when responsibilities inevitably pile on.

Julie M., a Director of Accounting, moved her entire family to France to accept a CFO position within her company. Her husband gave up his position within the marketing department at a top Fortune 500 Company, which helped them greatly during the move abroad. "Since my children were young and my husband was available to stay home during the first few months of our relocation, I was eager to take on the challenge. We found a great house to rent, a wonderful school for the kids and eventually, my husband found an excellent position as a marketing consultant at a local corporation. By then, we had childcare in place and the kids were settled in." Her husband's flexibility allowed her to focus on her new role as a CFO and helped her succeed professionally. They have remained in France for five years and even had Julie's mother move there to live with them.

And then of course, there is the matter of the partners' relationship. A strong marriage can succeed and even improve abroad, allowing two spouses to grow closer and take on challenges together. But those same challenges can cause rifts in a fragile union as two people realize they may have made the move too hastily. Amaire T., a clinical psychologist in Beijing, says, "Without the back-up support, the web of relatives, close friends, familiar locations and comfortable customs, the marriage is laid bare and a couple may for the first time see what their marriage is truly based on."

Christian B., a new hire at an international consulting firm, writes, "I knew my wife, Sierra, was excited about our move to London for my new job. We had talked about the romance of the city and how the journey could bring us closer together. But I also knew she was less than excited to leave her huge Texas family and her job. The transition was extremely rocky. We discovered it is illegal for Americans to enter the U.K. and begin job hunting without a work visa, but the process of obtaining a work visa could only be begun by an employer who could demonstrate why Sierra, an American candidate, fit the job better than any European Union candidate. It was a vicious cycle we just couldn't break into."

He adds, "To make matters worse, Sierra's family began to suggest, with good intentions, that she should come back to her family. They even went as far as to advise that she leave me. I was busy and she was lonely; we both were. We began to resent the process, resent our seemingly hasty move and unfortunately, resent each other. In short, our marriage was in trouble."

If the statistic mentioned earlier about divorce rates of expatriates didn't seem alarming, here is information that will: in addition to a myriad of other factors, including money strains, culture shock, and responsibility stress, many expat couples attribute disturbingly increasing divorce rates to infidelity. The sense of freedom that can come with living in an entirely new culture without extended family, lifelong friends, the fear of others finding out, and the daily routine leads to high infidelity rates among expatriates especially. Again, nothing can beat talking to your partner both before and after relocating.

Couples Survival Tip

Discuss expectations with each other and make it a point to **continue to share** concerns and disappointments, as well as the joys with each other on a regular basis. Trying to hide any concerns or pretending that you are fine just to avoid a short-term argument will inevitably backfire when those stressors reach the tipping point.

But don't let this doom and gloom persuade you away from the possibility of expatriating. The fact is that many failing partnerships simply aren't prepared for the changes that the marriage will undergo at home or abroad. Sometimes it just takes work. Remember Christian B.'s predicament in the U.K.? Eventually, he turned to his company and EAP for help. "I called the EAP first. They really understood and provided a list of marriage therapists in London who could help. We didn't even end up going. I just used some of the techniques I was taught, such as being more proactive about my communication and to focus on our shared goals.

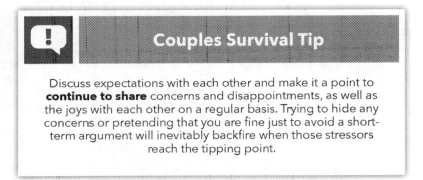

"My company really helped as much as possible. A consultant from my company helped Sierra write a European-style resume, learn the ins and outs of the local job market, and prepare for interviews. Within a couple of months, an airline company was interested in hiring her and was on the way to getting her a work visa. And when Sierra started working and socializing again, the waterfall of complaints from her family members slowed to a trickle. Our love life flourished again."

Still have concerns? That's normal. If you and your partner work through things as a united front, there's no reason the partnership shouldn't survive and succeed abroad. Use the following guidance when making plans for expatriation while keeping the family and partner relationship in mind.

Family To-Do's

Discuss with your partner why you each want to move abroad and what you expect to get out of it. Your reasons don't necessarily have to line up, but being aware ahead of time will prevent heartache if expectations fall through.

Each family member can recognize and come to terms with their own concerns through lists, family meetings, joint internet research and reading about the country that will be their new home.

Take advantage of any and all training and resources provided by the organization before and after relocating. They are there to help you.

Remember to consider your family's needs. Adaptation experiences aren't easy – take time to talk things through, recognize each other's feelings and emotions, and provide support. Religious contacts, friends and other expatriates may provide helpful suggestions.

Develop a habit of keeping open lines of communication between you and your spouse. If you find this is difficult, plan a time, once per day or at least once a week, to sit down and share each other's joys, frustrations, concerns, triumphs and lessons. Any deeper concerns about the safety of the marriage may be brought up during this time, as long as both remain willing to listen and problem-solve. Make a pact now to remain open with each other throughout the move.

Cross-Cultural Parenting

It's hard enough to raise a kid in one culture, but in two or more? Impossible, right? While it might seem like a daunting task after the initial honeymoon period of being in a new country wears off, rest assured it is not impossible to raise children in a synthesis of seemingly conflicting cultures.

Steven was eight when his parents, Mark Q., a physician and Lori Q., a travel writer, decided to make the move to India. He quickly made a fast friend, seven-year-old Bansi. As it turned out, he was equally fascinated with superheroes and action figures. Though they didn't speak the same language, they were inseparable, until one incident broke the bubble of intercultural harmony. "We came out into the yard one day and it was chaos," Lori remembers. "The neighbor's dog was hiding under the porch with his tail between his legs, Bansi was screaming with a bloody gash on his head and Steven was nowhere to be found." When Bansi's parents came out of their home, the situation got even messier. Without a clear language to communicate in, it was uncertain what exactly had happened and who was at fault. How did they get it sorted out?

"We found Steven hiding around the corner and marched him inside to give him a stern talking-to, but Bansi's parents insisted their own son was the culprit. What were the cultural rules here? How could we discover the truth about the mismatching stories when we didn't even have the words to explain? Whose fault was it and how was fault even determined in India?"

Eventually, Mark went to the neighbor's house to bandage up Bansi's head as a peace offering. Separately, the boys nervously told their parents the story. It was a made-up game they had been playing, one in which Steven had been "shooting" at the "villainous" dog and had missed by a mile, accidentally hitting Bansi with the makeshift weapon instead. Though Mark and Lori were embarrassed on behalf of their son, the incident raised many questions about cross-cultural parenting. Would the neighbors be offended by how they had handled the situation? Would Bansi and Steven still be allowed to be friends and play together? How could they discipline their child when they could not even find the cause of the issue at hand and how could the parents communicate and be friendly with one another after such a situation?

Cross-cultural parenting befuddles the lines of what parenting *is*. Parents might find themselves grappling with raising American children in a foreign land. "We had every intention of spanking Steven for recklessly hurting someone," Lori remembers. "But how could we tell Bansi's parents not to give him a sound whack with a wooden pole?"

Other parents may find that similar problems may challenge the way they've dealt with parenting in the past. Ben O., an engineering consultant in China, says, "One day, my eight-year-old daughter came home and started telling me everything about the new kids at school and I mean *everything*. She rambled on about how old their parents were, how many children were in their families, where they came from as well as highly opinionated gossip that went along with it, and how much money they made. "Hannah, it's not very nice to talk about people when they're not around," I said gently, more than a little concerned about how much information this little spy might feel compelled to divulge about myself. "Oh, that's alright, Dad," she informed me with what would prove to become one of her very first, and certainly not last, eye-rolls. "I traded vital stats. And they wanted to know how much money you made?" "I was floored," recalls Ben. "My daughter asking *me* for my income so she could trade the information like some commodity on the schoolyard playground! And to think, all I traded growing up was secrets about who liked who!"

Ben faced a twofold dilemma. On the one hand, he knew that such behavior in Michigan was unheard of. When Hannah grew up, if she was to eventually survive in a cross-cultural workplace, whether staying in China and speaking with business people of either culture, or returning to America, she surely couldn't be allowed to gossip about strangers' income and personal lives. But, for now, the behavior was being reinforced at school by children and parents alike, and would be reinforced in the culture she was growing up in. If she didn't adapt, she would likely be considered rude by the current culture and be denied access to certain social or business opportunities.

Expatrients, a term used to describe the parents of expatriates, find themselves straddling cultural lines to give their children the best of both worlds, without the inevitable confusion it can lead to. Third Culture Kids, or TCK's, are those growing up across cultural boundaries. For TCK's, their cultural identities are constantly in flux. They may feel as though they can travel through two or more cultures, but lack a sense of belonging in either one. "Where are you from?" becomes an anxiety-inducing question. Growing up, TCK's have been known to lack commitment. Mila G., a young adult recently repatriating from Spain, says, "Sometimes I was left feeling utterly powerless about my own life. From choosing a university to something as simple as sending an RSVP to a friend's birthday party, I was directionless and to a certain extent, I still am. I don't know if I will even like living in the U.S. after living away for so long. I don't know if I will move back to Spain because my family's here. Every plan for the future feels like a promise I'm just going to break."

Third Culture Kids create a sort of "merged" culture, fused entirely of the child's own making, a potpourri of positive and negative experiences from each culture. It reflects on a *betweenness*, walking the line but never taking up banners for any one side.

Identity crises are not uncommon. "Who am I?" can't easily be answered if one's sense of values cannot be determined. Do we put high value on family, as many South American countries do? Do we value respect to elders as in some Eastern countries? Do we value hard work or the end result more? Independence or tradition? To become the best person they can possibly be, TCK's must first decide on the ideal qualities of a human being, and those ideal qualities vary widely between cultures.

For some, that may mean camouflaging. Make-believe is a wonderful game for most children who reside permanently within one culture. For TCK's, it's a survival skill. Pretending to be confident with the customs of cultures and subcultures, when in actuality a child may be feeling confused and lost, is a game that TCK's are experts at. They feel out the temperature of the room, quickly learning the values of the people around them and how to communicate. This is one of the factors that may lead children and later adult TCK's, to undergo an identity crisis. When children "change skins" too often, how can they ever define who they are?

But while children, and later adults, struggle with a sense of identity, they can ultimately be more valuable in terms of social structures and business. "A little bit of my heart will always be in Pakistan," says April P., whose parents were spiritual directors there. "It's hard, always longing for a place no matter where you are. But it was something that made me unique. My peers were curious and I suddenly became the expert on all things foreign in the classroom. Now, I have an experience that is part of the reason I was hired to work at a huge multinational corporation. It's my goal to be assigned in Pakistan soon."

As she discovered who she was and came to terms with her multicultural identity, April realized that her peers truly didn't understand her. "They didn't ask any questions below the cursory. In a way, Pakistan was like my own little secret, with all my experiences and memories kept close to my heart. As I became more confident,

I knew my place in the world wasn't a place at all, but a state of cultural fluidity, an identity that was uniquely me."

April's parents said they didn't notice she was struggling until after they had returned to the United States. "She seemed fine. She was always upbeat, glad to be back. Yes, she said she missed Pakistan. But I didn't know how much she was having trouble fitting in. When she finally made some real friends, they were all from immigrant families. April identified with them because she felt like a stranger in her own homeland."

All troubles are relative. Third Culture Kids can benefit from parents who are open to communication and who encourage integration with the new culture while still providing boundaries and structure. Expatriates are, by nature, nomadic, multi-cultural and adaptable. But structure can help a child feel secure and free to explore him- or herself. Even something as simple as a Minnie Mouse cake helped one expatriate child feel closer to home. "Tara was turning three while we were in Pakistan," Penelope U. said. "Specialty cakes are big in America and the process usually involves cake tasting, design selection from a large book of samples and ordering at least two weeks in advance. In Pakistan, the process involved my mother-in-law picking up the phone, asking for a 'Minnie Mouse' cake and hanging up. I said, 'What about the flavor? How many people will it serve? Is it going to be a Minnie Mouse head or the full body?'

"She simply said, 'Inshallah,' which means 'God willing,' and basically means to leave it up to fate. 'It will be fine. He is a baker, so he knows what to do.' And we didn't check on that cake again until delivery," Penelope notes.

"The guests had arrived, the buffet was served, and now, it was time for the big cake reveal. We anxiously opened the box to a chorus of gasps, not of wonder, but of shock and horror. This was no Minnie Mouse cake. This was some regular old chocolate round cake. Someone had drawn a smiley face with tacky red lips and two circle ears on it. It was as if the baker did not even look at a picture of Minnie Mouse and just started drawing whatever image came to mind and went with it."

"It was too late to try to salvage the wreck. My family was already singing 'Happy Birthday.' But the truth is there was not a crumb of cake left because it really was delicious. Ironically, all the guests asked for the baker's contact information at the end of the night. It reminded me of how in America, we can go to the extreme with trying to control every outcome and make our kids happy by any means necessary. But, while we're focused on 'Are you going to give Minnie Mouse a pink bow or a red bow?' most people just want to eat some good cake."

Not everything has to be perfect. Sometimes, the effort is what counts. Family rituals and traditions can provide just the structure that expatriate kids need to both remember where they came from and learn where they are going. "Will Santa know where I live?" bemoaned one young child when Christmas time came around. Children, strangers in a strange land, can be appeased and comforted if there are rituals they can anticipate, events that can be planned and counted on, in the nomadic life.

One family managed to keep their old traditions while integrating with those of the culture during the holiday season. Adora H., having grown up in a military family, says, "I remember at the beginning of the Christmas season in Germany, my parents told me to leave a shoe outside of the house to see what Saint Nicholas would put there. They would say, 'This is how you know what you are going to get for Christmas -- twigs if you are bad and sweets if you are good.'" Sound similar to our coal-and-candy traditions in the usual stocking? "Of course," Adora adds, "I was the sweetest daughter, so I always knew I was going to get sweets." Traditions help children feel grounded, at least in family culture.

A tradition doesn't have to be something as big as a holiday. Family rituals might be invented by the parents. "We were back and forth across Europe for years," Jade E., a mother of two, says. "My oldest daughter was fascinated by foreign coins when she was younger. It turned into a tradition of going to fountains, tossing a U.S. penny in and taking a native coin out for keeps. Now we do that no matter what city we're in. When we first move, we hunt down and map the fountains where others have left their good wishes and add to our collection. It's something the girls can look forward to no matter where they are, leaving a piece of themselves and taking a piece of the country with them when we leave."

"My kids have become experts at scouting out the markets for substitutes of American staples," says Finn K., who expatriated to Turkey five years ago. "Once a month, we have a real 'American' dinner that they get to cook, but the adventure lies in trying to find the ingredients. We've had ground lamb instead of beef, really hot spices instead of salt, pita instead of buns and a really sharp cheese that I pretended to like instead of cheddar." The three children are nearing their mid-teens and though one doesn't have much interest in cooking, he does like to participate in chowing down the "meal from home." "We were huge hamburger fans before we moved," Finn admits. "It was hard getting used to the foreign food. But whenever we have that monthly 'American meal,' my belly feels like I'm at home."

And what about when children have questions about what is appropriate? "Use your judgment," Ben O. (the one whose daughter had some pretty nosy friends) says. "Ultimately, it's your house your kids have to be living under. You want to provide some structure of normalcy and you want them to value the qualities that you also value. But, you also don't want to alienate them from their peers by forcing them to ignore standard cultural customs. What I eventually told Hannah was that it's okay for her to set boundaries with the other kids at school. I would advise her to say something like, 'I'm sorry if I seem rude, but where I come from, we don't really talk about family finances.' And I encouraged her to find some other, safer common ground with them."

"You have to be strict if they're in a public school," Eloise P. says. "They're not with you during most of the hours of the day. All of their new friends will be teaching them about the new culture, which is great. But, when you do have time with them, you have to make the most of it, both as a loving parent and as a teacher."

"Kids are smart," Logan J. said with a shrug. "Maybe they struggle at first, but they'll learn to navigate going from culture to culture. Mine did."

Adora H., whose Christmas traditions helped her stay grounded in the family, really benefited from being a TCK. Her experiences helped her to more easily adjust in an increasingly global workplace. "I developed an appreciation for different cultures and learned how to adapt to my surroundings. This is why, when I was a junior in high school, it was easy for me to live in Australia and New Zealand for two months during summer break as a sports volleyball ambassador. Playing volleyball overseas and representing the United States, for my age level, was an incredible experience. I have to credit my ease of transition to living abroad at a younger age."

So, what did Lori and Mark end up doing about the awkward cross-cultural situation with their son and the neighbors' son? "Steven and Bansi were equally traumatized by the event and for the moment, no further punishment was necessary. Soon, the boys were back out in the garden again playing superheroes. They have forgiven and forgotten and are apparently over the drama of cultural hang-ups. They still don't speak the same language. Long story short – we still have a lot to learn."

Parenting To-Do's:

The benefits of living abroad as a family are sharing many great adventures and becoming experienced world travelers. If your family can focus on the positives, they can use this time in their lives to enrich themselves as people.

All children may assimilate to living abroad differently. Be open to concerns and questions. If you don't know the answer, be honest.

For example, "I'm not sure what our home will be like in Japan, but I know we will all figure this out together."

Act as a team to bring the family closer. Conduct internet research as a group. Learn the language together and start speaking it at home. Practice the metric system, if that is the measurement system in the country you are relocating to.

Develop some fun family traditions that can be as easy as taking photos in front of each house you stay at or seeking out the cities' best ice cream spots. Children will look forward to the tradition and experience a little bit of normalcy amidst all the moving.

Foreigner or Foe?

Think about the army of comrades who have got your back right now. There's the friend you can call with any problem, 24/7. There's the grocer who knows you by name because you've been going to that same grocery for 20 years. What about the neighbor across the way who picks up the kids from school when you're running a little late? How about the friends who come over every week to watch the game, or the friends who show up just to say hello. And of course the indispensable coworkers who cover for you when you're out sick.

Now, imagine your life without any of these people, at least until you get settled in. New expatriates do not have the luxury of shared place or shared history with the people they encounter day to day. It's not just a simple move – expatriates also encounter the divide between culture and language. The most well-adjusted Americans overseas will build up that support network rather quickly. Even if they can somehow create a culture of supportive, helpful people for themselves, in the back of their minds is always the irksome thought: *We're not here forever. I can't afford to make lasting relationships. Once we leave, we'll never see each other again.*

One problem at a time. Yes, in this increasingly digital age, it is easier than ever to stay in contact with loved ones, near and far. Just because your best friend used to live two blocks away from you and now lives five thousand miles away doesn't mean you have to cut off communication completely. Nadia N. recounts, "My daughter was living in Barcelona for the entire semester, but with Skype and Facebook, she might as well have still been in college locally. We talked almost every day and she posted pictures of her adventures weekly. I felt included in her travels and I think she felt closer to home."

There is a great way to share your experiences with the world, and that's blogging. Just run a quick search on expatriate blogs and you'll have access to thousands of first-hand experiences of travels abroad. Au pair (nanny) Heather from Atlanta created her own travel blog with regular updates and pictures, so her family could subscribe and receive articles on her life in Turkey with her host family, and send her comments and encouragement. She described her visits to the bazaars and Turkish coffee shops. She shared stories of the children she was caring for and teaching English. Heather networked and socialized with other nannies during her free time. The au pairs continue to stay in touch since returning to America.

Some expatriates will take this to an extreme: "I don't need local friends! There's the Internet, video chat, smartphones, texting, blogging and so much more! I'll always be in contact with all of my old friends." That might be true to a certain extent. Certainly the closest friends from home will want to check in once in a while, but the fact remains that nothing trumps face-to-face interaction (or living in the same time zone). One blogger realized that after five years abroad, the relocation was taking a major toll on her home friendships. Without shared experiences and the commonality of place, she had fallen out of touch. Until you make that new network of contacts who are there to catch you should you slip, you will never feel truly at home. And yes, home is exactly what you want this overseas experience to feel like. How else will you maintain a new normal?

When feeling disoriented in a foreign culture, some expatriates will cling to the familiar. They socialize only with fellow expatriates and withdraw into their carefully-constructed dwelling places, maintaining minimal contact with local people. The support network of a like-minded expatriate community can be great for new expatriates just learning the ropes. "My husband and I moved to Wuhan, China only about a month ago," says Elise C., a U.S. Culture instructor. "One of the first things I did was look for any expatriate communities in the area. The only one I could find was called 'Women of Wuhan,' and while my husband didn't go to that first meeting, due to the group's name, I met two really wonderful couples. 'I can't believe you joined us so quickly,' one woman, who soon became a close friend, said. 'We spent our first two months lonely and miserable before this group.' Really, this is the best thing that I have done for myself since arriving and I expect this expatriate group will continue to be invaluable as I learn the language and culture." There's nothing like finding people who understand being in the same situation. Local expatriate communities may be able to introduce you to the local cuisine, the best schools or most affordable clothing in town and any other tricks of the trade. Why reinvent the wheel?

Networking Tip

From the start of your trip abroad, develop a network of personal and professional contacts. **Devote time and energy into connecting with others.** Having local relationships and friendships will be important to you, for the duration of your assignment and beyond.

Charles S., a working student traveling between the United States, Japan and Germany, struggled with making local friends. "I have a lot of people that I like to mingle with, most of them acquaintances but very few who know me well," he said. "To them

I was a novelty, a guy with a funny accent and a funny worldview. The vast majority of my conversations with them involved explaining how Americans could possibly think the way they do about politics and laughing when I didn't know something about their culture or history. It was all in good fun. While they were just being friendly, it started to wear on me after a while."

Others embrace the challenge of living fully in an unknown culture, interacting with as many people as possible. This is more difficult and requires the expatriate to stretch out of that comfort zone. Wrapping yourself in an expatriate cocoon won't help you assimilate very easily and may actually increase stress. You aren't going to live exclusively indoors in some ivory tower. Social interactions with members of the local culture play a significant role in expatriate satisfaction. Introduce yourself to everyone you meet. Depending on social hierarchies, it's a good idea to build some friendly relationships that can buoy you to safety during stormy expatriate seas. Workers abroad feel truly at home when they have that kind of support system, not only of fellow expatriates, but of people who call the host country home.

Making friends abroad turned out to be a very positive experience for Andrea S., who was in Cairo for over a year working with a major retail outlet. "My dearest memories of Cairo are the friends we made there. I was amazed at the amount of English spoken, the general friendliness toward Americans and the invitations. Dining in other people's homes gave me tremendous insight into the country, its amazing culture and rich history. The internet has allowed us to stay in touch with those friends although I have not visited Cairo in three years."

Spencer B. describes firsthand his impression of Dublin: "I was greeted by American friends when I relocated but quickly learned that English was not the same in all English-speaking countries. I had to ask Dubliners to repeat what they said two or three times and was constantly asking about the vernacular and dialect that seemed like a foreign language from what I was used to. When I was not with my American friends, I had never felt so lost." In this case, Spencer's dependence on his American friends inhibited him from adjusting to a different dialect, making the move that much more difficult. Yet, it was a welcome stepping stone as he adapted.

Where and how do you meet great locals? Depending on the cultural circumstances, some people may consciously stay away from foreigners, especially in the early days when expatriates haven't gotten a grasp on the customs. You may inadvertently do something rude, such as stepping into a house without first asking, "*Con permiso*" (with permission) in Ecuador. You may be barraged with stereotypes or negative perceptions of American culture. Or some locals may be disinclined to make friends with expatriates, knowing from experience that foreigners will likely be moving on too soon.

The lesson here is to keep trying. Persistence is the key to success and success is not something that will be handed to you on a silver platter. Even something as simple as chatting with a street vendor or accepting a neighbor's invitation to dinner can slowly help you to meet new people and integrate with the culture. Below are some common ways for expatriates to be introduced to locals who could very well become lifelong friends:

<u>Kids</u>. If you have children and have brought them along for the ride, they are a natural and easy pathway into the culture. Mingle with other parents at your children's school or social activities.

<u>Class</u>. If you find yourself having some extra time, consider taking a course in a hobby you love, whether it be a book club, pole dancing, joining a local football (soccer!) team, or joining a poker club. You'll meet like-minded individuals who share your passions.

<u>Volunteer</u>. Nothing could be better for you or for the community than hiking up your sleeves and helping out alongside other well-intentioned locals.

In some cultures, friends might be almost simple to find. Again, disparate cultures come into play. Elizabeth L., a working mother in China, says, "I remember very clearly going out to find a taxi with my three youngest kids. It was freezing cold. No taxis stopped. But a couple of guys on motorbikes did stop and tried to offer us rides through the hectic traffic. They were really nice! But it took me several tries to get them to take no for an answer. Another elderly gentleman offered to walk us across the street where it was easier to get taxis. He patted my children's heads as though he was their own grandfather. Now, in the U.S., we helicopter parents might quickly usher our children away with a brief 'don't talk to strangers' lecture. But here, it's totally normal. I've gotten used to exchanging 'idle chat' with strangers. Everyone is incredibly friendly and seems genuinely interested in conversing. Some of my best friends I've found while talking to strangers at the markets."

Adjustment to anything takes time, and temperament plays a huge role in one's ability to slip easily into new friendships. We may not all make friends as easily as Ellen DeGeneres, George Clooney or Joey Tribbiani. But everyone *can* make friends and those friendships will not only help expatriates feel more at home, but are likely to last a lifetime. As one expatriate, Adrienne L., remembers, "I have few friends who know me very deeply, and that includes friends from home. After three years of living in the U.K., I married my husband. It was spur-of-the-moment, with no invitations to anyone. We grabbed a hand-holding couple off the street and asked them to be our witnesses. One week later, they married and we were invited to be theirs." He was a Brit who loved hotdogs, the Raiders and advocated for the American version of "The Office." She had been adopted from China at age two and gushed incessantly about British politics, cuisine and fashion.

"The friendship simply *was*. And even though they moved away a year ago, they're still our best friends. I sometimes drive three hours one way on the weekend to see them and their babies. We still celebrate holidays together. It's not the same, living so far away, but even if my husband and I were to move back to the United States, I know that we would be lifelong friends, no matter how many miles are between us."

Adjustment doesn't happen overnight, so be patient. Practically speaking, "cultural informants" – locals and other expatriates – can get you on the fast track to understanding your new environment and making you a happy, healthy expatriate.

Friendship To-Dos:

Don't be shy! Introduce yourself to your neighbors. Most will be more than happy to provide a few home-cooked meals, local gossip, and advice on the best grocery stores or schools. More likely than not, they too know what it's like to feel displaced.

Join a local organization, either professionally or for a hobby. It's a win-win way to meet new people. Introduce yourself to some professional contacts while beginning to create a solid foundation on which to build this new life abroad.

Local friends not getting you? Slow down, take time to listen to what they say, and empathize with their worldviews. Remember, as the Prayer of St. Francis (and later one of Steven Covey's *Seven Habits of Highly Effective People*) says, "Seek to understand rather than be understood." *You* are a new change to *locals'* environment, not the other way around. Being understood will come later.

Accept that loneliness is an inevitable part of the experience. We will all have moments or even days of loneliness, but chances are, someone out there is lonely too. Find them and befriend them.

Be open to new experiences. Accept invitations and let the 'comfort bubble' around you shrink until you make direct contact with those around you. But remember to be safe!

And – you guessed it – look over the 3 R's when considering family life abroad.

The Three R's of Stage 3: Settling In:

Recognize that each person in an assignment has differing priorities and expectations. Take time to evaluate what family members expect to get out of the move and what their concerns are. If one member of the family suffers, the entire family suffers. Establish goals and work to keep communication honest and open.

Respond by addressing the needs of family members and friends as they come up. Not everyone has to be on board with the move and not everyone has to have a splendid time 24/7 once you get there. Difficulties always arise. Take care of your needs and be sensitive to other's concerns.

Reinforce by practicing open communication with new local and expatriate friends. Generally, patience and acceptance in all aspects of life go a long way when trying to cope in a foreign country, while impatience and intolerance are counterproductive to the unique expatriate situation. When something goes wrong, be patient with yourself and seek not only to understand the situation, but prevent it from happening again.

LIQUOR &
PERFUME
WHOLESALE-RETAIL
CHINA
sparky's
LIQUOR
SPECIALS

BAR
BAR

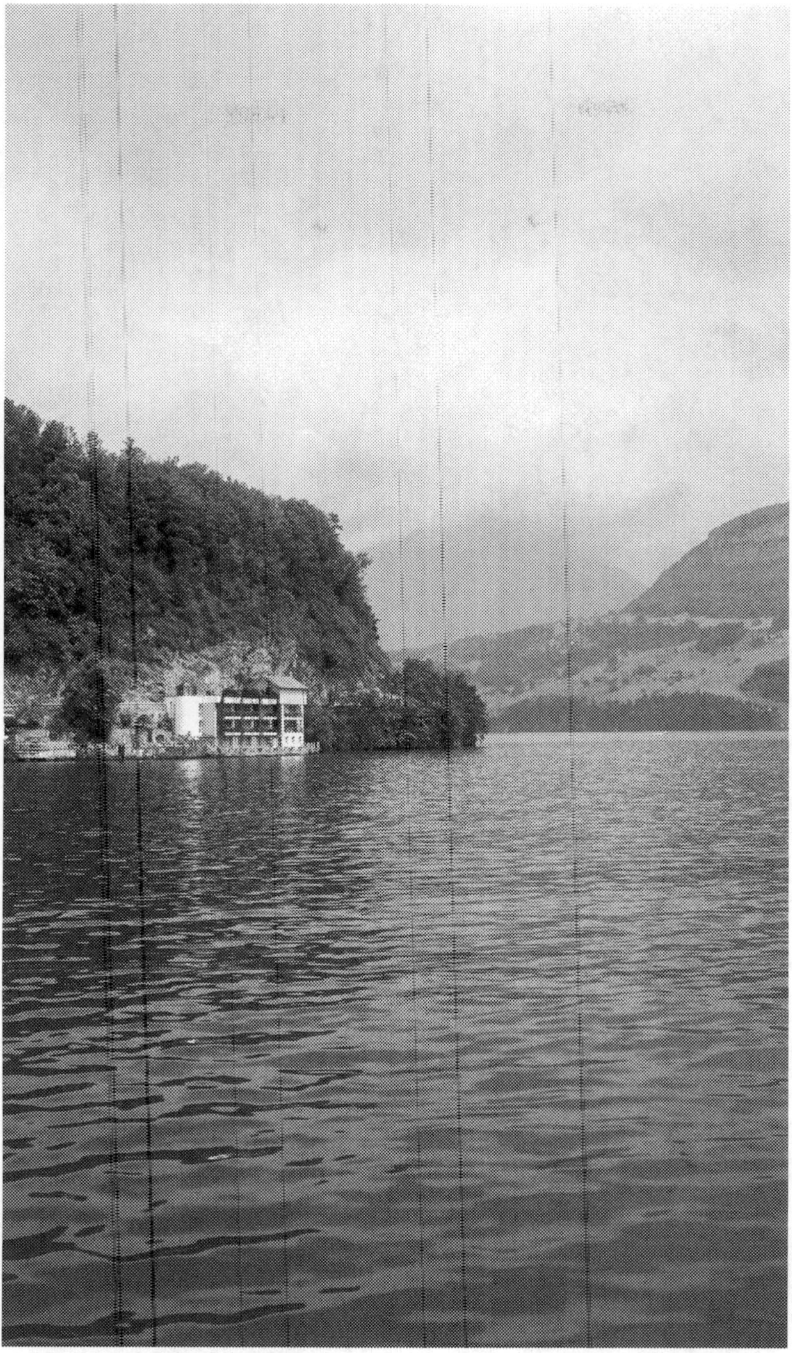

NATO FIORENTINO
DE SIMONI

YAMAHA

Stage 4: Adjustment

"The real voyage of discovery consists not in seeking new landscapes, but in having new eyes."
- Marcel Proust

A common reason for expatriates to repatriate is finding the challenges of adapting to everyday life in their new country just too daunting and hard. Go in with an open mind, remain patient and know that not everything makes sense in any nation in the world. You are the only one who can change your own mind and your own tolerances. You can't alter the psyche of a nation.

You can do a lot to help yourself adjust. Remember that whether feeling lonely and homesick, or struggling to navigate around town, you are not alone. There are plenty of people you can go to for help. Maybe an older relative has experience visiting and working abroad. Maybe a close friend is the only one who will listen to your sorrows. Or maybe your EAP with international reach can help you find local specialists trained in culture shock and adjustment. Sometimes, we just need to hear some advice or that our experiences are normal.

Anne D. from San Diego shares her experiences traveling to Africa. "On my first visit to Morocco, among like-minded Americans in a tour-guided pack, I had promised my friends some great souvenirs like pointy-toed shoes and sequined headscarves. We found those, but we found something else as well. 'Look at this pretty fabric!' I heard a man say, followed quickly by a pitched scream of horror. A woman was shifting anxiously from foot to foot, staring at the gutters as rivers of blood ran down the street. We got a few irritated looks and some laughs as the butcher, right next to the boutique shop, waved the leg of a dead pig."

American shoppers know this is not the normal experience in the states. "I had not expected to see fresh meat so close to the tourist trap. Swarms of flies flitted around. Beggars crowded the kiosks. But it was just that--a shock. I quickly realized that what I was seeing was standard. We get American pigs in prepackaged sausages, but at some point, they must have looked like these bloody butchers' carcasses. What I was seeing was just a worldwide daily chore, hidden from view in my homeland, but casually open and on display in Africa."

Inexperienced expatriates can be taken completely by surprise at the deep cultural differences in their host country. The lesson here: Learn to adapt.

Stranger in a Strange Land

The title is from Robert Heinlein's science fiction masterpiece. A human, raised by Martians, descends to Earth and becomes a stranger in his own homeland. Doesn't that parallel how we feel when traveling anywhere that isn't within our own comfort zone? At first it seems like everyone around us is alien, acting and reacting in ways so foreign they might as well be from another planet. We chuckle at their outlandish customs. And then, slowly, it becomes clear to us that we're the aliens in this strange, foreign land. Should we give up when we don't fit in?

Once the novelty of living in a new country wears off, the excitement of living in a strange environment will become just that - strange. Inevitably, we start to feel overwhelmed, tired, irritable or anxious. Perhaps at work, we don't feel we are making the great strides we expected to make or that we feel are expected of us. Partners at home may be feeling listless, lacking in direction, enthusiasm or purpose. Our children seem unsettled, life is suddenly not so rosy and we begin to wonder, was it all a big mistake? For a small minority it may well have been, but for the great majority those experiences are perfectly natural reactions to the big change they are experiencing in their lives – a predictable response to entering a new and uncertain environment.

The term "culture shock" is a good label for the psychological experience of adults during the time of cultural adjustment that accompanies a period of socialization or acculturation. The cultural adjustment period usually includes some disorientation.

Widespread conformity can be a bad thing. If the world was all the same, what would be the point in travel, adventure and diversity? Most of us move abroad to experience challenges and opportunities, for excitement and enlightenment. But the reality of moving to a new culture and settling in can be quite a long way away from the dream of how easy it will be. Even the most open-minded expatriates will be challenged when they come into contact with strange local behavior, complex red tape and seemingly mindless bureaucracy. But isn't our own home town equally filled with odd and peculiar encounters? Think how outsiders might react to Super Bowl riots, the Department of Motor Vehicles, or even the eccentric people at the local Wal-Mart.

Mark L., an American citizen born in Luxor, Egypt, was transferred to a Dublin automotive company. Since he spoke English and had traveled widely, he felt well-prepared to live in Ireland - wasn't it almost like America with an accent? But the reality was quite different. "I wish I had taken the opportunity to find out more about what was in store for our family. I took too much for granted because the Irish seemed so familiar. Every American seemed to have Irish roots. I only heard about the positive aspects, but not the stress, worry, anxiety and the loneliness. For all its similarities, it was still a foreign country nonetheless. If I had taken the opportunity to learn more about the different cultures that existed within Ireland, I would have been better prepared and maybe realized that these feelings and experiences are normal."

The sneaky psychological symptoms of culture shock can camouflage themselves as normal periods of loneliness or frustration. We tell ourselves that these feelings are temporary and they are. We tell ourselves we can handle anything as long as we stick it out long enough. But then we start getting ill-tempered with our loved ones, withdrawing from local interaction and emphasizing our criticism of local customs. Something is out of balance.

Culture shock affects the whole person--mind, body and spirit. The symptoms of homesickness and culture shock are very similar and are often interrelated. The mind is working to encourage the body to return to the familiar. The mind then presents thoughts that things will be better elsewhere. Keep in mind the acronym for FEAR: False Evidence Appearing Real. Here are some examples of how the expatriate's mind could be exemplifying these fears:

- Unwarranted criticism of the culture and people
- Heightened irritability
- Constant complaints about the climate
- Frequent excuses for staying indoors
- Idealizing one's previous culture
- Continuous concern about the purity of water and food
- Fear of having close contact with local people
- Refusal to learn the language
- Preoccupation about being robbed or cheated; safety is an ongoing concern
- Preoccupation with returning home
- A sense of overwhelm and helplessness
- Homesickness and a sense of loss
- A dip in self-confidence
- A sense of being rejected by or rejecting the new culture
- Mild depression/anxiety; even mild paranoia
- Irritability and hostility towards the new culture and its foreign practices

Ian H., a Canadian businessman moving to Chile, admitted, "I became really depressed. I didn't have the same support system that I had back home. My job was getting me down and I didn't have my usual coworkers to rely on. I began to question my desire to move to Chile. Worst of all, I began to question my own self-worth." His experience is not uncommon. He couldn't seem to adjust quickly enough and placed blame on himself as a result. His serious lack of equilibrium within himself was causing problems in every aspect of his life. He did not have the necessary, healthy state that is "a dynamic fit between parts of the internal system and external realities – that is, an attainment of internal coherence and meaningful relationship to the outside world."[11]

How do we cope with culture shock so we can maintain this healthy state? Having some information about culture shock is a first important step. Attempting to distance ourselves from ethnocentric perspectives will help. It is also important to normalize stress. We're all veterans of stress, and culture shock essentially is stress, just in a different location.

Normalizing the experiences of a foreign culture is a major part of the experience. Some authors view the phenomenon of culture shock as having differing phases. The honeymoon period is that of falling in love with the sights, sounds, smells and smiles of a new country. "I remember vividly my first view of the Hong Kong skyline at sunset while riding in a romantic rickshaw," recalls Dana P. "That was quickly balanced out when the very polite but rigid hotel clerk could not find our reservations, which were well-confirmed and made far in advance."

Once the honeymoon is over, the next phase may be seen as a negotiation between you and the differences that you must accept in the new country. After some time (usually around three months, depending on the individual), differences between the old and new culture become apparent and may cause anxiety. Vanessa L. fell

---

[11] Kim, "An Integrative Theory."

victim to this when she and her husband were in their first week of Permanent Change of Duty Station in Brad Kreznauch, Germany. "My 10-year-old daughter really wanted to go swimming in the hotel pool. So I dug her bathing suit out of the luggage and she went on her merry way, happy as could be, to the pool. I had planned to follow her in ten minutes, but as soon as I was heading out, she came back screaming! I asked her what had happened and she managed to blubber, 'Mom, there are all these naked men in the pool!' Mortified on her behalf, I had completely forgotten– my mind was still in the United States, not in Germany."

Adventure and romance may eventually give way to unpleasant feelings of frustration and anger as one continues to experience unfavorable events that may be perceived as strange and offensive to one's cultural attitude. Physical reactions to culture shock, language barriers, traffic safety, food safety, accessibility and stark differences in public hygiene, may heighten the sense of disconnection from the surroundings. Brittany F. realized her sudden fear: "I can't even eat out – how will I know if everything is cooked? And what if someone takes my purse at the restaurant?!" Such reactions are normal. But, we could get food poisoning just down the street at IHOP or get robbed at our favorite places at home. What's the difference? The unknown is always scary. Those experiencing culture shock will gradually make accommodations, adaptations and yes, change. Acceptance is the key to more quickly becoming "a part of" instead of "apart from."

As an example, Westerners aren't generally used to clothing restrictions in general public. But Qatar's recent "One of Us" campaign brought to light just how often it is that expatriates and travelers are completely unaware of their cultural insensitivity. The poster shows four photos of "immodest" clothing, ranging from sundresses to tank tops and the caption: "If you are in Qatar, you are one of us. Help us preserve Qatar's culture and values, please dress modestly in public places by covering from shoulders to knees." "I wasn't even in control of what I wore," said an exasperated Portia

E., whose husband was recently transferred there. "This basic personal freedom was taken from me. I caused a scene as one mother murmured to her child about this 'foreigner' dressing the wrong way. I had been wearing a sundress on one of Qatar's hottest days. I felt trapped in my own skin."

When we are suffering from culture shock, we usually feel out of control. Don't spend energy on things you cannot change. Instead, enact change where you can. Pamela J. was being transferred to Ukraine. Her anxiety was so high that it was starting to reflect in her job performance. She was trying to learn all she could about the new country, which only added to her anxiety.

Her EAP counselor suggested she focus on her wardrobe. She laughed. When she returned for her next session, she was a relaxed and happier patient. She began by telling how foolish she thought the suggestion was. Then, when she couldn't sleep for yet another night, the suggestion clicked. She began to take clothes out of her closet, make lists and organize her shoes. She had taken control of what she could control.

And what about Portia who traveled to Qatar? "One of my coworkers sat down with me after I'd apparently been complaining a little too loudly. 'That is just the way it is here,' she explained, much more patiently than I deserved, I'm sure! 'You would not run around in your underwear where you're from or maybe you would! But we don't go around in our underwear here.' Wow, did I feel foolish when it was put that way. And here I was teaching my children about what I thought was modest!"

Eventually, the final phases of adjustment do come. Routines develop. You begin to know what to expect. The patterns of basic living take over. Things begin to feel normal again. Problem solving becomes a way of life. The culture, with its customs and eccentricities, begins to make sense. And soon, you begin to see the positive side.

Laura D. who visited Pakistan writes, "One of the strangest things to adjust to in Pakistan is the help around the house. Every upper-middle class family basically has live-in servants, as well as a driver, a gardener and a housekeeper who work every day of the week. There is a much larger discussion to be had about the lack of class mobility and segregation in Pakistan. But for me, it was bizarre to be surrounded by 'help,' but at the same time, feel so 'helpless.' If I wanted a sandwich, I pretty much had to ask for it. If I wanted to go somewhere, I had to be driven. And with a house full of people, privacy is very limited and doors were constantly revolving. While most upper-middle class families speak English, the 'awam' or working class, typically speak Urdu, Punjabi or one of the other Pakistani languages. You can imagine my sign language and broken Urdu must've looked ridiculous when simply asking for a towel for the shower."

"With time, however, we adjusted to a rhythm, where communication and daily interaction became much easier. They started asking me questions about America and I got to hear their stories. I was most struck by how happy and content they seemed, even in the face of what most would consider pretty hopeless living situations. One girl, Nagina, was helping watch the babies and she was only 14. I learned that before working at the house, she was actually picking peanuts for a dollar a day. I remember how she would watch me put on makeup or how she would admire my clothes and shoes. I wondered what I could do for her. But she never walked around in a 'Why me?' sort of way. I actually have a lot to learn from her. The connection I had with the working class in Pakistan truly opened my perspective, challenging me to live differently and more gratefully."

Jabilla W. had described her experience in Argentina as "going native" and thought she must have presented a comic picture with her red hair and freckled skin, screened, hatted and protected from the sun. But, after some time there, her empowerment had come. She began to see the host country in a very positive light and find herself frustrated with her home country. "I began to see that there were better ways of doing things. America seems so dependent on packaging and ugliness. I saw in this small city in Argentina that people carried net bags and totes. In that moment, America just seemed small to me and I became so angry at the waste and the lack of gratitude I felt toward my native land." Jabilla went on to say that she hoped to be a force for positive change when she returned to America by working with nonprofits to get more paper and reusable bags available in stores.

Elyse C. ran the entire gamut of culture shock when she moved to Germany. "I remember feeling very conscious of how different I was. America and Germany are similar in a lot of ways, but it seemed I stuck out like a sore thumb everywhere I went. People would laugh at me for making mistakes, like pronouncing things wrong or having a funny philosophy and I would kick myself for messing up and eventually stopped interacting, afraid I would mess up again. I would downplay my differences and try to become more 'German.'"

"But, after a rather embarrassing encounter in what I had no idea at the time was the German version of the Red Light District, I realized that I sucked at being 'German.' I couldn't pretend that I liked paying so much more in taxes or watching rugby. Trying to *blend in* was not helping me *fit in* at all. In fact, it was hiding my greatest asset--my differences. When I started embracing those differences, I was more interesting and memorable and it opened a lot of doors for me both professionally and personally. People *responded* to my difference. My advice for expatriates: Be culturally sensitive, but be authentic. Be you."

By taking actions that focus on positives, the mind will begin to support change. Make sure each day includes some fun for you and the family. Maybe it is simply going to see a movie or indulging in a delicious American treat. Fun is fitting in. As you become more relaxed and enjoy where you are, your mind will work creatively to understand and embrace the new culture.

Adjustment To-Do's

Normalize the experiences. It is important to know that experiencing culture shock is not a sign of weakness, but more a sign of personal awareness.

Take the culture in small bites. Establish routines before trying to conquer your destination country. Begin with short walks in familiar neighborhoods. Smile and be friendly, but don't stress about speaking the language with finesse until needed. Slow and steady can be reassuring.

Prepare for ways to handle the negative effects of stress from the start of your life abroad, such as quickly establishing your exercise routine and squeezing in relaxation time. There is always one more box to unpack and one more word to learn. But relaxation will only happen if you plan for it. Remember, the word recreation is really re-creation; the creation of energy by removing stressful activities.

Something embarrassing is bound to happen. Laugh it off and be patient with yourself.

Be aware and sensitive to cultural differences. Ask questions rather than take offense.

Keep in mind this golden rule when dealing with rude behavior: Outsmarting and outmatching others won't work in foreign countries when they are the ones who are on home turf. When in doubt, don't react.

Focus on what is in your control. If you can't control everything all at once, start small, like organizing your closet or find a reliable routine like morning chats with neighbors.

Rather than giving up your culture so you can fit in, keep your mind open to new ways of doing and thinking about things. Notice things that are the same and things that are different. Appreciate the diversity that makes people and cultures so interesting, while still preserving your own.

The Language Barrier is Real

Not knowing the intricacies of pronunciation in French, Ynes O., an American nanny, picked up a new puppy for the children she was taking care of. "*Chiots*!" she told the children excitedly in French, just as their mother walked in the room. "Puppies! I love puppies." The children immediately broke out into red-faced laughter and their mother's face grew very stern. "Apparently," Ynes recounts, "you are not supposed to pronounce the hard "T." I had accidentally told my charges that I loved poop!"

Language is the number one challenge among many listed by expatriates while living and working abroad. Most attempts to learn the local language are meager at best. Recent trends show that expatriates are making greater efforts at language assimilation and also are better at learning foreign languages than in the previous decade.

Humans need social interaction to thrive. We are community-orientated animals that need contact and stimulation through communication. Expatriates struggle if they cannot effectively communicate in the local tongue. While some may meet other expatriates or locals who speak English, the majority of expatriates can find the language barrier to be an incredibly detaching experience.

Not everyone finds it easy or even possible to learn a foreign language well enough to communicate effectively. This can lead to isolation, loneliness and a deep homesickness that could drive expatriates home. "I tried at first," says David V., an architect who relocated to Brazil. "I thought because I already knew Spanish, that it would be easy to learn Portuguese, too. But I struggled every single day for something as simple as asking for local dishes without cheese. Eventually, I started to give up and isolate as I kept to English or Spanish-speaking expatriate forums online."

The way an adult learns a foreign language can affect the way their brain processes the language. Those who undergo immersion, where they are completely surrounded by all aspects of the language, tend to have brain processes similar to that of native speakers. By linking a word in the new language to the actual thing, rather than linking a word to its English counterpart, an extra step of translation is no longer necessary and more native-like thinking will slowly form. For example, *perro* signifies a furry four-legged animal that barks, rather than signifying the word *dog*.

Although learning a second language as an adult is notoriously difficult, full language immersion can lead to more native-like attainment; "The possibility that explicit (classroom style) training may hinder the development of native-like grammatical processing is intriguing and warrants further examination. It suggests that even though explicit training might provide early advantages, its longer term consequences may not be so beneficial."[12]

Failure to learn the new language relates to many of the other problems expatriates can encounter. For example, one study on German expatriates ranked "finding new friends" as a top-ten challenge for 72 percent of those surveyed[13]. Benito J. spoke about his own efforts in France. "People told me the French were snooty and cold. I found them very open and accommodating to my poor efforts at speaking their language. But I began to realize how I treated tourists in America. I live in Michigan and tourists are a part of the landscape. But, I never thought of making friends with one. Then I realized in Michigan, I had my friends. The same is true where I am in France. They already have their friends."

---

12 Clancy, "Immersion."

13 "Expatriate challenges."

Language Tip

Don't be afraid to ask your company to pay for the tools to help you learn the local language. Everyone learns differently, so if the computer programs don't work for you, try a local tutor, or audio programs. There's an app for that too! Get the family involved. Encourage each other to **speak your new language at home**. Have someone teach a new phrase at dinner each night.

Many schools have language classes. More impressively, the internet has opened up many different opportunities for learning. App-based language lessons on your phone are the norm nowadays. DVDs with headphones can be useful while multitasking. Hire a tutor and combine touring the new area with everyday language.

It is important to seek out English speakers in the early stages of your settling-in. There will be plenty of times during the day for you to practice your new language. Finding English-speakers may reduce the initial culture shock and help you gain confidence as the many other challenges of resettling get handled.

Whatever method you choose, practice makes perfect. A lot of people worry about speaking a language they aren't completely comfortable with. What if native speakers tease us when we stumble over the words? This might tempt you to practice the language with someone who is at the same comfort level as you, but it's also important to practice with people who have mastered the language, so that you know when you make a mistake and learn from it. Those who know the native language will appreciate your attempt to speak it and are more likely to be more lenient when you make a mistake.

It might make you uncomfortable when it takes you twice as long to say the same thing as a native speaker or use the wrong word altogether. Remember, many foreigners grew up in a much smaller country with shared borders. It is common for children to grow up in multi-lingual environments. Picture each state in the U.S. as having a different language. Give yourself credit for your efforts. Small steps lead toward big progress.

Even if you're familiar with the new language spoken around you, chances are you haven't picked up on much of the slang yet. "This is really embarrassing," says Nolan B., an expatriate in Australia. "I said I'd been sitting on my fanny all day. After a long, uncomfortable silence, someone was good enough to inform me that 'fanny' means something else entirely in Australia. I had very loudly told them that I was sitting on my vagina all day." This is one of the many reasons why it's a good idea to do some studying on the culture you are immersed in and spend lots of time with native speakers in order to bolster your learning and more swiftly adjust to the culture.

Other parts of the language may be strictly culture-based. "You think that Italians have a reputation for talking with their hands and over-exaggerating," says Derek P. "But Mexicans have them beat. Every sound has a different connotation. 'Uyyyyy' and 'Ayyyyy' have very different meanings and different emphases depending on how many hand claps go along with it. My friends would laugh when I tried to mimic them. But I laughed too and it was all in good fun."

Language Tip

Read the papers, watch TV shows, get a language tutor, join a gym or after-work social group, and get help from other expats. Communication in business is critical, and **immersion helps**. Even if the locals speak English, work hard to learn the new language.

And a final bit of advice--keeping up a concerted effort to learn about language and culture takes some discipline and determination.

But every step toward being able to communicate in a foreign language, every act of engagement with life around yourself, and every instance that shows you are trying to the best of your abilities will be reciprocated with a sense of achievement and growing confidence.

Foreign Language To-Do's:

Do something, every day, no matter how small, to learn the language. Get a pack of grammar flashcards and go through them once before breakfast. Have a conversation with one of the waiters at a local restaurant. Read a short article out loud or watch a local TV show without subtitles. Mix it up to keep your interest.

Don't be afraid to make mistakes out loud. Every mistake is an opportunity to correct and learn.

Seek out local language groups, usually part of expatriate communities.

The Law of the Land

Did you know that it is illegal to chew gum in Singapore or to drive a dirty car in Moscow? Did you know the penalty for masturbation is decapitation in Indonesia?

Aside from the culture shock, foreign laws can be disorienting, restricting and sometimes enraging to people who are used to abiding by American laws. Time taken to research laws, especially those visiting Americans often have trouble with, will prevent much frustration and may even prevent expatriates from possible foreign imprisonment, a quagmire of complications in itself. Laws vary widely from country to country. Often, corporations will provide expatriate employees with information regarding what is expected of them in the new country and in the workplace. Training, information and other services will greatly improve an expatriate's chances of having a safe and successful stay abroad. Additional resources from embassies or official travel websites may provide the information needed.

Penelope M., who moved to the Netherlands to work as an educational consultant, ended up staying there and discovered one particular American custom was absent from her new home. "I was so excited to get married and take my husband's last name, but it turns out things are a little different here. Even if you get married, you still legally keep your original last name with a formal suffix only used, apparently, for letter writing. So I'd be breaking the law if I signed my husband's last name on holiday cards!" She had to adjust her vision of how her marriage would be presented to the world and subsequently adjust how she told people about the circumstances of her last name.

Americans are used to the freedom to practice whatever religion they please. It was one of the founding principles of the country after all. But be careful when openly practicing in foreign countries. Even simple displays of faith such as wearing a cross pendant or a yarmulke, may be frowned upon in other countries. "In Saudi Arabia, the birthplace of Islam, it is against the law for Muslims to abandon their faith, a practice known as apostasy. Proselytizing for other religions or practicing them openly is also illegal," says an article in Arabian Business[14]. That's what led two men who converted a woman to Christianity to receive prison sentences and hundreds of lashes.

Sometimes laws may be even more pervasive, affecting not only how we dress but how we communicate. Recently, in one of India's eastern states, cell phone use by women was banned following a series of elopements and extramarital affairs. Those caught using cell phones on the street are required to pay a fine. "It's easy to be angry about things like that because it's just unheard of in the United States," Jenny adds, referring to her own similar experiences. "But the fact is that they live their lives differently. They have a very dissimilar culture, with its own shared history almost completely separate from our worldview. The best thing to do is to go along with

---

14 Reuters, "Saudi Arabia."

it, realizing that as an expatriate, my stay here is limited anyway. It's still important to learn as much as you can about the culture. Find common ground with locals. Chances are there's something that you have in common, despite our differences."

American-related laws will vary if an expatriate moves abroad. In addition to income taxes of the host country, taxes based on citizenship must also be paid to the U.S. government, whether or not the expatriate's organization resides in America. Citizenship requirements will not change for expatriates. You can still vote via an absentee ballot and receive all the rights of an American citizen, but children of expatriates might encounter difficulties voting and gaining American citizenship, especially if the child was born in the host country or if one parent is not a U.S. citizen. Also, Medicare compensation is not currently available to U.S. citizens living overseas, but Social Security may be, with certain stipulations. Visit AARO.org (Association of Americans Resident Overseas) for more detailed information about American laws applicable and specific to expatriates.

A good rule of thumb is, when it doubt, don't. Don't use a cell phone if no one else around you is using one. Don't pop a bubblegum bubble if you see no one else chewing gum. Once you are more clear about the laws and regulations, legal and cultural, you can afford to take a few more risks, just not *that* many! Be prepared for changes in laws with the following to-do list.

Legal To-Dos:

Research, research, research. Look up local laws on transportation, taxes, food, housing, education, work and more. It's impossible to be fully prepared, but do your best and be ready for challenges when they arise.

Find a local contact who is well-versed in at least basic host country laws. Having this resource can be invaluable in preventing any potentially embarrassing situations.

Stay in touch with American voting results, changing laws and regulations, especially as they apply to citizens working abroad. You'll especially want to be up to date if you repatriate to the United States.

Can We Go Home Now?

Some of us thrive on adventure and some of us just think we do! You'll find out quickly when giving life abroad a real go. Like a kid at camp, when the newness wears off and the lights go dim, thoughts turn toward the comfort of home. It is part of the normal expatriate experience to miss home, friends and family.

After the confetti has been thrown and the farewell hugs completed, communication with those at home may become just another chore. Skyping requires an appointment. Emails become too long or too short. The experiences are all new and exciting, but sharing them may reduce the fabulous sunsets, sandy beaches and good food to clichés. The phone calls may seem lopsided as you describe the many adventures and amazing sights, while family and friends report "not much," or "same old, same old…" And unless you were born a natural storyteller, there's no way to convey the emotional intensity of finally communicating with someone in a different language or getting lost on darkened streets with no one to call.

Soon, you find that one of the mainstays of friendship is sharing a common lifestyle and interests. When you move offshore, your lifestyle changes significantly, often in ways that your friends and family can't visualize. They may disapprove of or even be jealous of how you live. Friendships may lose their depth, their intensity and shared feelings. You begin to realize that while these friendships may be forever, they will never be the same as before you left to undertake this opportunity. Not only are you missing them, but you may feel you are vanishing from the hearts and minds of those you love. Sometimes the exchanges are about things you have missed - the marriage of friends, the birth of a baby, a graduation, a friend who needs your help, a divorce… The lives of you and those you care about gradually diverge.

Mandy L. missed her best friend's wedding. "I guess I thought she'd wait until I got back. We even talked about it. The next thing I knew I was looking at pics on Pinterest. Even my invitation arrived after they were back from their honeymoon. I know it may seem like a small thing, but I really cried and my husband couldn't see what the big deal was. It made me feel so alone."

As one expatriate, William G., living in Sweden, writes, "These are some things that I have learned. Most people will not understand the incredible amount of suffering involved with moving abroad. You lose everything at once- your home, your friends and your environment. You are expected to start functioning again as if nothing has happened. It is impossible to love a city the way you loved your first. You have no past here and not much of a future. It is impossible to feel completely at home. Something will always feel off. And yet, despite all of this, you learn. Life goes on and you start to appreciate everything around you in a new light. You build a new home with new memories. You thrive."

The distance doesn't seem to present a problem, until it does. When a loved one becomes ill, you can't just gather your belongings and leave at a moment's notice. When your grandfather suddenly passes away, you may not be able to attend his funeral. When your best friend is getting a divorce, you won't be at her side. Whatever the reason, there will be many times when you want to be home and it simply won't be possible. There will be many more times when you just need a hug, a quick pick-up game on the basketball court, a couple of beers or a round of Cosmos with a rerun of "Sex and the City." Sorrows and joys, bereavement and birth can all be shared virtually. But it's just not the same.

Lane W. says, "I never thought about the Super Bowl. I mean, I had thought about my parents and accidents and stuff like getting sick. Who would have thought about the Super Bowl? Well, I did. I went to a supposedly American bar in Brazil and there was still only soccer on the TV. I just couldn't stop thinking about how it should be me and my crew and I kept saying, 'Man, it's just a game.' But it wasn't just a game. It was a piece of home that I couldn't have here."

Expatriate flu is a myth to those who have yet to make the move abroad, but after three months or three years, most expatriates will experience it. It is a physical manifestation of the stresses, concerns, negative feelings and worries that all expatriates have at one time or another.

With symptoms similar and interrelated with culture shock, most expatriates experience expatriate flu after about the first six months or so. The initial euphoria dies down when the reality of living abroad has much in common with living at home. There are bills to pay, chores to be done, children who require special attention and a certain level of stress associated with settling in, living and working in a new environment. When we're ill, we feel vulnerable and helpless and for expatriates, the first time they really go down with a bug, virus, cold or flu, it may cause us to question our commitment to living abroad.

Confidence Tip

Don't second guess yourself or your decision to move abroad. These negative thoughts can be debilitating and snowball into self-sabotage. If you find yourself questioning "Why did I do this? What was I thinking?", remember your mission statement. Mentally reiterate your reasons for making the move and **remind yourself that you are living your dream**. Try to pinpoint the causes of your doubts and address them directly.

A period of homesickness is inevitable for almost everyone. One term is "island fever," a feeling of claustrophobia and a desire to get away from the perceived isolation. Sometimes this feeling simply requires more action on your part--using the tips in this book to become more acclimated to the culture, find friends who can make you feel at home, and further settle in. Sometimes, professional help is needed.

This is a time for reaching out to the many sources available to you and other expatriates. It might be something as simple as comfort food. When Sandra got homesick, she found that one thing always made her feel better and was available in nearly every country she traveled to– McDonalds! "Not all locations even served hamburgers, which was a shock at first. But there were always fries, that faithful comfort food."

Culture shock can have a huge impact on feelings of homesickness or loneliness. Strange things are bound to happen. Daily life might seem surreal as it becomes more difficult to get accustomed to a new normal.

As Sarah C., whose fiancé is a flight attendant for an international airline, remembers, "Keller gets to travel to some amazing places. When he was going to Dubai, he asked me if I wanted to use a buddy pass and come with him. Of course I said yes– who would turn that opportunity down? But we hadn't done our research and when we arrived at the hotel, we ran into an enormous problem. We were not allowed to stay in the same room together because we were not married. How embarrassing! We ended up getting separate rooms for the month-long trip and I had never felt so lonely in my life. Keller was my home and something I had taken for granted."

These feelings could have been minimized by proper planning. The importance of pre-planning has been stressed throughout these chapters. But here you are and the feelings may be overwhelming. Here are a few tips to keep in mind when combating homesickness associated with relocation and culture shock:

Homesickness To-Dos:

Educate people about your culture. Just because you're the one entering the new culture doesn't mean you should be the one doing all the learning. Take the opportunity to acquaint peers and new friends with your culture. They may already know some things about it, but teaching them about the food, traditions, laws, viewpoints, music, etc. of your home country will also help them learn more about you in the process.

Be sure to debunk any stereotypes associated with your culture, especially if you're American. Who knows? Perhaps your impression of their homeland is just as skewed as their impression is of yours. Be sure to address and tackle those myths early on.

Invite them over for traditional dishes from your culture or show them how you celebrate your holidays. Why not have a Thanksgiving turkey in *Noviembre*?

Find a support group. Expatriate groups are common in most countries. You can share experiences, cheer each other up when things get rough and introduce each other to the new friends you've made. Again, the internet is a vast source of information.

Make it easier to keep in touch with home. Skype, text, Facebook, free messaging apps– choose your social medium du jour. Write letters and e-mails, and make an occasional phone call so you can stay up-to-date on the things happening there. You've not only left behind people, but also things like your favorite spot to hang out. Keep pictures around to remind you of home.

At the same time, don't obsess over thoughts of home. Follow previous tips in this book to interact with new friends, neighbors and colleagues, and embrace the local culture and country as your new home for the time being.

You Are Not Alone

If you've been reading this chapter and fretting over everything that needs to be done, researched and planned, don't worry too much! There are literally thousands of resources at the disposal of expatriates abroad. These resources should be utilized for expatriates' best chance of succeeding in a work situation, in a family, and in a new culture.

Employers have everything to gain from an expatriate's success and everything to lose from a failure. They should be invested in an employee's stay abroad. Utilize any pre-departure training that is available and be sure to reach out to the HR department or to the local EAP for briefings, support and resources. Though some employees may feel uncomfortable asking for help, rest assured that this is a sign that an employee is actively interested in achieving success for him or herself, and for their company.

Countless resources are available on the Internet. You just have to know how to filter them. Below are some popular expatriate websites that might support these overseas quests.

- *ExpatExchange.com* - A kind of social network for expatriates, this website is full of information about culture shock, living abroad, jobs, finances and more. Talk on the country-specific forums with other expatriates in the area.
- *EasyExpat.com* - Job listings, a cost of living calculator, blogs and classifieds are just a few of the topics you'll find covered on this all-encompassing expatriate guide.
- *ExpatForum.com* - A worldwide forum to exchange stories, advice and news with other local expatriates.
- *ExpatNetwork.com* - Often used for finding overseas jobs and careers, this site also serves as a search engine for communities and provides financial advice across borders.
- *ExpatWomen.com* - With great resources for expatriate communities by country, and a number of interviews and testimonials, this site offers insight into the unique challenges women face working abroad.

- *FutureExpats.com* – Great personal-account advice on the planning side of working abroad, including portable careers, preparing to move, resources and more.
- *InterNations.org* - Get to know like-minded expatriates locally. This is the world's largest resource for connecting with real-life people and fitting in to the local culture.
- *OverseasDigest.com* - With a plethora of first-hand accounts, articles and job opportunities, this website features hundreds of resources to help expatriates choose a career and prosper abroad.
- *TransitionsAbroad.com* - With articles, guides and advice about living, studying and working abroad, this website will be sure to have something for every expatriate.
- *USA.gov/Topics/Americans-Abroad* - The United States Government official site detailing the ins and outs of legal, health, work and travel technicalities for working Americans.
- *WorkPermit.com* - A popular immigration advice website, with access to forms and information about the technicalities of working in another country.

It's important to be yourself. Try not to force yourself to change too fast or to try too many things all at once. You will have your own pace of adjusting. Everyone goes through ups and downs in their life and it may seem that you are going through more changes than the average person. But as long as you hold on to what's important to you, you can find a good combination between old and new. Remember, the key to getting over symptoms of homesickness and culture shock is to understand the new culture and find a way to live comfortably within it, while staying true to the pieces of your home that you value.

The Three R's of Adjustment

Recognize that the foreignness is normal. That shock and anxiety will go away in a very short time. By building routines and acceptance, the mind and body will give up resistance to change.

Respond by fitting in relaxation time. Set aside time for small walks to familiarize yourself with the neighborhood. Join a health club. Free up family time to visit local sites. Plan activities with other English-speakers for a break from thinking in a new language.

Reinforce by rewarding yourself for trying new foods or making new friends. Set realistic goals at work that give you time to assimilate all that is new. Reward yourself each day for your accomplishments in learning a new word or just making the effort to speak to a local.

Stage 5: Achieving Success

"Travel is like an endless university.
You never stop learning."
- Harvey Lloyd

Throughout this book, we have suggested three action steps for success in each chapter: **Recognize, Respond** and **Reinforce**. Now, it's time to take a big-picture look at how you, a valuable member of your organization, can really excel in your new environment.

How do we define success? Is it determined by how much money you make? How about the number of local and expatriate friends you have? Or the number of followers on your blog or Twitter feed? Remember those goals you set at the beginning of your assignment, before you ever moved abroad? It's time to revisit those. Your goals will differ from each of your peers. Maybe you wanted to hold your own in a conversation based in a foreign language. Maybe you wanted to get a promotion at the end of your assignment. Maybe you went in with very few expectations and your experiences far exceeded anything you could have hoped for.

Success will mean different things for every expatriate. You should measure success against your own goals. But what if you just couldn't get a grip on the language? What if you didn't get that promotion? What if every imaginable problem befalls you and you just can't wait to get home?

Believe it or not, there's success in that, too. There's something to be said about failure, which I think gets a bad rap. People usually *regret* failure. It's not fun when we fail. We question our self-worth and decision-making skills. "If I had just left well enough alone and stayed at my job at home…" But try to think of failure as a learning experience. If you're miserable in your foreign assignment, congratulations! You've just learned that you don't want to live abroad, at least not in that country. Think of it kind of like tasting the Japanese delicacy *shirako* (fish sperm). Some might get sick at the thought. Some might feel repulsed at first, but be adventurous enough to try it. Without that risk, there is no reward. Think of these experiences as trial-and-error situations. Tried it and erred? Stick with the rice and miso soup next time.

The point is this: **Don't be afraid to fail**. Risk-taking can yield real results and separating your work from ideas of perfection will help you be more flexible and grow as a person and as an employee. Congratulate yourself for the risks you have taken so far, good or bad!

Let's get back to the keys of success.

Recognize.

"In 2004 I took a chance," remembers International Relations Specialist Ryan W. "I knew it would extend the amount of time I would spend in school and the loans I'd have to pay back. As an expatriate kid, I'd be uprooting yet *again.* But, I had always wanted to visit China. "So I took a semester through my school to travel there. And you know what? I stayed. I finished up school here. I got a job at a Chinese company as their official ambassador to the United States. And even though my parents weren't too excited, I've never been happier."

Learn to **recognize** success when you see it. It might be as grand as realizing you want to live long-term in the country you are expatriating to, or it might be a list of small wins. Here's an example list of little successes you might experience:

Resolved an argument in the country's native tongue

Made a local friend

Kept inside the budget for the first month
Received praise from a coworker or boss
Recovered from an illness
Went on a fun date with your significant other
Laughed at your little mistakes
Picked up your happy child from school
Wrote and published a funny blog post

Life almost never builds up to a climactic scene in which you run through the airport for the last flight back home. It isn't always as dramatic and clear-cut whether you've won or not. Events accumulate and contribute to your happiness with your foreign assignment or your unhappiness. Take a close look at those little telltale signs that you are succeeding.

You should also be able to recognize where there are areas for improvement in your life abroad. If this book has advocated anything, it is to be open-minded in overseas experiences. Be gentle with shortcomings and work to improve them.

"I would beat myself up every time I got laughed at for pronouncing something wrong," says Emile O., a teacher on sabbatical in Honduras who volunteered to teach English. "The students laughed at me and the other professors would make harmless little jokes. But it really hurt me. I said I was sick for a week and instead hid in my room, listening over and over to tapes in the Spanish language. But it didn't help. It was when I actually did get physically ill that I realized the language barrier was affecting me more than I thought. It had really crippled me, to the point where I created lesson plans that allowed me to speak as little as possible. I talked to my boss about it and she said a lot of foreign teachers had the same problem."

Recognizing our shortcomings is the first step to success. If Emile had never recognized what the problem was, he might have gone home early, feeling confused and frustrated with himself and the experience.

Eventually Emile talked to the right people and used his international EAP service to get coaching on how to approach the students who laughed at his accent. He started taking control of his environment. But for some, recognition might mean something else. It might mean realizing that you don't have the patience for a foreign assignment, or that your values lie elsewhere. Maybe your family is struggling to cope and your marriage is more important than your life abroad. There's no need to take action yet. Simply recognize what problems exist. Make a list. Analyze from there where your priorities lie.

"Writing is a great way to track the internal chatter in your brain," says Celeste Gertsen, Ph.D., a clinical psychologist[15]. Everything can feel overwhelming without perspective. So try it. Spend five minutes and write everything that comes to mind– your struggles in this new land, your triumphs, how you feel about what you ate for breakfast, how you missed your niece's birthday or even the weird conversation you had with a stranger on a trolley. Write everything down. If you think you want to repatriate, focus on that as you free write.

Now, your issues should seem much clearer or at least, a little simpler to understand. Take some time to look over and reorganize them into a list or create a mind map, a visual representation of how your thoughts are related. This can be a great way to recognize what exactly seems off and then work to correct it.

After trying this exercise, Felicity M., an account manager in Berlin, said, "I never realized before how much my dissatisfaction with my job came from my fear of losing it. I was good at my job and loved the work, but I would still worry every day that I would be laid off since the big company reorganization the year before. I had written down these telling words- 'I'm not doing my best at work anymore.' And then I thought, why? And I wrote, 'Why should I try so hard when I'm just going to be fired?' There was really no reason I should be fired, but that fear was limiting my ability to succeed

---

[15] Hall, "Think it," 166.

and love my work again." Thankfully, Felicity was able to **recognize** her fears and what was really preventing her from thriving in her foreign environment.

Respond.

Lingering over thoughts, no matter how valuable, will have no impact without action. Everyone will admit that change is tough. Deciding to take action is tougher, especially when you're not sure of cultural norms. But, you'll get nowhere if you don't **respond**.

"I don't want you here," Shania's Saudi-born boss said. "You aren't right for this job. You aren't going to fit in and you don't have the background for it."

Shania had heard that Saudi Arabia was a notoriously difficult place for women to live and work, especially foreign women. Yet that hadn't stopped her and her husband from securing jobs and traveling there, as much for the adventure as anything. But she stood still now, facing her new boss, the male manager of a small school. Shania mustered up her courage and met his gaze. "I know that I have a lot to learn, but I am a team player and I have come to work very hard to teach these students. The longer I am here, the more I can contribute."

Her boss studied her with hard eyes and then turned to walk into the building.

Shania realized she still had a job, but the men in her building were extremely formal and her manager did everything he could in an attempt to prove that this western woman was not suitable to teach there.

Determined to succeed and prove her worth, Shania took over a few extra shifts when one of her male colleagues fell ill. Her manager was surprised to find her in the classroom so late in the day. "What are you doing here?!" he accused.

Shania smiled and replied, "Teaching."

"But it's not your time to be here. You are on the incorrect schedule."

"I know."

The manager stalked out and Shania continued to teach the classes throughout the next day. The next morning she was called into her boss's office. *I'm going to be fired,* she thought, *but not without a fight.* She planned what she was going to say to defend herself, that she had only been doing what was right, that she wouldn't ask to be paid for those hours she'd covered for her coworker, that she'd take on extra shifts if need be.

She stepped into his office and before she could get a word in, Shania's manager said rather harshly, "Would you and your husband like to come to my home for dinner tomorrow night? My wife will be cooking lamb and falafel."

Shania was floored. Here she thought she couldn't ever be up to standard in her boss's eyes, but he had noticed how hard she was working and had appreciated the effort she was putting in. The dinner turned out to be wonderful and over the next two years, her manager became a friend.

Shania had recognized the circumstances she was up against. She realized that it would be hard as a western woman to assimilate in this patriarchal society. But instead of giving up out of fear of failure, she pursued the career she wanted and worked hard to prove herself. Overall, Shania's **response** helped her win over a friend.

Responding can be something as straightforward as taking more initiative at work. It can also be a lot more complex when you're not exactly sure how to respond to a seemingly unfixable situation. What happens when you miss an important flight? Or when the kids come home from school a few months into the assignment and still aren't fitting in?

"I have that problem," says Erik W., an account manager in France. "I know it will take time for Philip to get used to his new school. He has always been a middle-of-the-pack student, though he's never come back with failing grades before. But what worries me more than his grades was his lack of friends. I asked him if he liked it in Marseille. He was reluctant to answer, but finally he just said, 'Dad, I don't get it here. Nothing makes sense and nobody likes me at school.'"

How does a parent **respond** to that? While Philip needs time to adjust, Erik does not want to ignore his very clear struggles. Erik settled in just fine. He had a job and coworkers waiting for him, but his 10-year-old son Philip has none of that. He started to feel guilty and unsure about his move abroad. How can he help his son succeed?

The best way to respond is to **START SMART**. This method is the simplest way to set clear goals, work to achieve them and respond when something goes wrong.

START SMART	
Set a goal	**S**pecific
Try it out	**M**easurable
Assess your success	**A**ttainable
Rework and reframe	**R**elevant
Try, try again	**T**ime-bound

Set a Goal

Erik can't succeed if he continues to wait, hoping Philip will somehow figure it out himself. Maybe he would, but what about the consequences if Philip doesn't get his feet under him? Would Erik have to move back home so that Philip would get the schooling he needed? Erik decided to get help with setting a SMART goal:

Specific, Measurable, Achievable, Relevant and Timely. He spoke with Philip and they worked through the steps together.

Specific – At first Erik suggested that Philip try to make more friends. But the goal is so vague that Philip didn't know where to start, especially because he had just started learning French the year before. He ended up more frustrated than ever and with a big test coming up, Philip began to isolate. That's why setting goals works one step at a time, in small increments, that eventually lead to success. Erik said, "Finally I did some digging and learned there was an after-school tutoring program."

Measurable –We want to be able to measure the success, or lack thereof, of our goals. Otherwise, how will we know if it worked? Erik added, "If the tutoring worked, the teacher told me that she thought Philip would be able to get at least a *bien* (equivalent to one of our Bs) on his big test."

Achievable – Our goals should reflect reality. They should stretch us just enough to be challenging, but not impossible to attain. "Philip was really opposed to it," Erik said. "He said that tutoring was for 'dumb kids.' But I know him and I know what he can do when he puts his mind to something. Best of all, the tutoring sessions would give me a little extra time to have a real meal ready for when Philip got out of school. I was going to try to make this feel more like a real home for him, not just a quick stop in a hotel with TV dinners."

Relevant – Would going to a tutor make Philip fit in more? Was it part of the plan to help him feel at home? Or would it distract him from making friends? "He told me he was worried that people wouldn't want to hang out with him because he was in tutoring," Erik said with a sigh. "I don't know if that's true or not." The goal was to help Philip be more comfortable at school, both with his schoolwork and social life. But Erik new if he didn't get his grades up soon, he'd have an even bigger problem on his hands.

Timely – In order to measure the success of this newly-formed goal, the two had to have a time frame to do it in. After all, setting a deadline makes the goal more likely to get accomplished. "Phil's big test was a month away," Erik said. "So that was our goal. We wrote it down together and put it up on the fridge as a daily reminder: *"After taking tutoring sessions twice a week and studying hard, I will get a 'bien' on my test."*

Try it Out

Now comes the hard part. It's easy to set a goal and a bit harder to commit to it. Don't be afraid to fail. As Henry David Thoreau would say, "Go confidently in the direction of your dreams." That means taking risks and taking those shiny new goals out for a test run.

Philip complained about going to tutoring. He said he didn't need it and he wasn't learning anything. But Erik would just point to the goal on the refrigerator. The month wasn't up yet. They were still trying it out. They just had to try a little harder.

One day Philip's tutor called. "He's a good student," she said in thickly-accented English. "But he forgets what he learned in the last session. He seems unmotivated."

Remember that the path to success is not well-paved. It's not the safe or easy road. It's rocky and filled with steep cliffs and muddy ruts. Keep trying until the agreed-upon date set in the SMART goal.

Assess Your Success

"Well?" prompted Erik as he rolled the sausage-like *boudin blanc*, a favorite of Philip's, onto a pair of plates. "How did it go?"

Philip frowned, though he perked up a little at the smell of the food. He held up his graded test, marked with a big red "AB."

"Is that good?"

"*Assezbien*," the boy answered. "It's below '*bien*.'" He went to the refrigerator, ripped their goal off of it and tossed it in the trash. "I want to go home."

It would appear that the goal had failed. Philip had seemed a little happier at school, came home some days chattering about the funny things the French children said or what his teacher was assigning. But more often than not, he was listless as ever and waited days to do his homework, if he even did it at all. Was the tutoring working? "But it's better than you've been doing," Erik said encouragingly. "Not all our goals are going to come true immediately. We have to work at it."

"I did and I failed," Philip protested.

"No, not at all! You have been getting better." He set down the plates on the table. "Didn't your teacher say you were improving?"

"Yes."

"And what about Henri?" Philip had started participating in the daily soccer tournaments the students had formed, despite the language barrier. There, he befriended his teammate, Henri.

Philip nodded mutely.

"So," Erik said, clapping his hands and enthusiastically dicing up the sausage, "It's not a complete loss. Let's see what we can do to fix it."

Rework and Reframe

Erik called up Philip's tutor to see what he could do to help. Not surprisingly, she answered, "Philip would really benefit from some at-home reinforcement of the topics." So, making dinners for Philip a few times a week wasn't going to be enough.

"At first I thought, 'No way- I just don't have time to do Philip's work on top of my own,'" Erik recounts. "But then, I looked at that SMART goal again. I'd made a commitment as much as he had. So after work, I started sitting down with him and going over what he'd learned in class and in tutoring. Let me tell you, it was hard to get that kid to study almost all the time! But I promised him I'd sign him up for the next soccer league session if he showed signs of improvement."

Try, Try Again

After reviewing their progress, Erik set another SMART goal with Philip: *"After taking tutoring sessions twice a week, and reviewing what I learned every night with Dad, I will get a 'bien' on my next test."*

"But, if it didn't work the first time, it's not going to work now," Philip said.

"We're trying something new," Erik answered brightly. "And I'll be here to help this time. We can do this together."

They both had to compromise. Erik compromised working longer days and Philip compromised playing soccer. It worked! Philip came racing home after a long day of school, tutoring and soccer practice and waved a paper enthusiastically in the air. "I got a TB!" Henri and some of the other kids from his soccer team filed in after, grinning.

Erik smiled hopefully. "Is that good?"

"*Trèsbien!* It's better than *bien*!" Philip laughed. "She even asked me if I'd cheated!"

Erik's brow creased with sudden worry. "Did you?"

The boy laughed again. "No! My friends helped me study right before!"

Erik smiled. "Wonderful." He pulled the paper with their SMART goal off of the fridge. "We ought to have this framed!"

The real test of success is to see if we will continue to try, even if it doesn't work the first time. And before you can succeed, you have to START.

So what do Erik and Shania have in common? They both took their fates into their own hands. Shania refused to let others perceive her as lacking qualifications because she was a Western woman. Erik refused to let Philip's school struggles impede them from having a successful expatriate experience. They were both proactive in their successes. As an expatriate worker, a wonderful experience won't be handed to you on a silver plate. Sometimes you have to reach out and take it, and at times, fight for it.

Reinforce.

"Success is a system – not luck."[16] Cultivate a garden of success around you. Don't just wait for it to find you, because it won't. Lucky people work incredibly hard.

So when you do manage to hunt down some luck, study it with a scientific eye. How can you re-create those circumstances of success? Physical therapist, Sharon J., said, "After journaling my progress every other day for the first few months, I realized two things-One, that I will never learn how to cook fresh fruit without burning it, as they love to do here. And two, I usually feel most accomplished when I have something to look forward to after work like a drink with friends, a quick movie, or a jog by the beach with my dog. That way, I feel I haven't spent the whole day without doing something for me and it's easier to keep going through the workday, even when I manage to burn another round of bananas." Sharon's story reminds us to reward ourselves for good behavior. We need to train ourselves to seek success and then be rewarded for it. Sometimes, that's as simple as asking a friend to congratulate you once in a while. "Keep up the good work!" can be the simplest motivator.

We all set up small rewards for ourselves that can seem like bribery: "*If* I get this done, *then* I can go to the spa." "*If* I have one week without any major emotional outbreaks from the kids, *then* I can pay for a babysitter and take a day off." This technique can also be used on kids and significant others. Try something like this: "If we stay under budget for the next three months, then we can take a trip to Paris and splurge." All work and no play makes us all very dull and irritable.

However, be wary of bribe traps. If you're bribing yourself into everything, you'll forget to live in the meantime. "That happened with me," says Tony G., a repatriate from Germany. "Every Monday I would tell myself, 'Just get through this week and you can have a steak dinner Saturday and Sunday.' This went on for about two

[16] Clark, "Workplace Warfare," (2013).

months before I realized I'd gained about fifteen pounds and the only thing I looked forward to in the morning was a steak lathered in thick sauce." Remember, it's not enough to merely seek success. You have to replicate it. It's a constant battle uphill against the forces that will seek to work against you. Don't let them win.

Let's take another look at those goals we created in the 'Respond' section. Having goals is all well and good, but consider this quote from *Workplace Warfare*, "clarity comes from action, not thought"[17]. We have so much more control over our circumstances than we believe. Once we realize that power, we can take control of our destiny and shape it to our liking.

Long-term goals can be hard to look forward to. That's why "reinforcing" also means focusing on the here and now. Each day spent abroad should be viewed as a success. Mistakes are learning experiences. Feeling exhausted means you are building up your endurance. Remember, as Johann Wolfgang von Goethe says, "It is not enough to take steps which may someday lead to a goal; each step must be itself a goal and a step likewise."

Break goals down into small, manageable bits. That's how you'd eat an elephant and that's how you'll succeed abroad. Marty Q., an accounting manager who went to India in hopes of getting a promotion upon his return, says, "I remember feeling completely overwhelmed by my workload in India. Everything that could go wrong in the accounting department did, and this time, I didn't have anyone to put the blame on but myself. I was in charge of ten to fifteen people at any given time and if I didn't check their work, the numbers would invariably be off. And if I did check their work, I would end up not leaving myself enough time to finish my own." What did I recommend to Marty? Simply to start from his SMART goal – "*Be promoted to senior manager at the end of the two-year assignment in India*" – and work backwards, creating a list of possible steps as he went:

---

[17] Forleo, "Beaten by Self Sabotage?"

Steps Toward SMART Goal

6. Become promoted to senior manager at the end of the two-year assignment in India
5. Successfully move back to New York after two years in India
4. Earn the "Employee of the Quarter" award in my second year
3. Receive over 70% positive feedback on the new process from other departments
2. Implement intuitive, streamlined number-checking processes
1. **Build relationships with employees and develop a rapport with management**

Now Marty had six action steps that he could influence and had control over. By working backwards from the final goal, he could now start at Step 1 and work his way up to being promoted as a senior manager.

After this exercise, I asked him, "What steps can you do by next week? Tomorrow? Right now?"

The answer astounded him. "More than half!"

It's amazing how much control we actually have over our lives. Marty took the first two steps immediately and the rest snowballed from there. Marty didn't earn "Employee of the Quarter," but he did implement the new number-checking process and drove their feedback up. And guess what was waiting for him in New York when he returned? A glittery new promotion!

It was hard to get excited about action steps when the enthusiastic first months in Djibouti, Africa, began to wear off for Georgia A., a Peace Corps Volunteer. "I was doing really well," she writes. "I was really happy to be working here, learning the culture and meeting all kinds of people from all over the world. And then I started getting sick every week and just really missing home." Fortunately, Georgia went to her Country Director. "I tried to fix it on my own. I tried everything I could think of, but it just wasn't getting any better and I was barely functioning at my job. I realized it would take a lot of courage to admit this." Georgia added, "But my Country Director was so understanding. He sent me to the next town over to practice relaxation techniques and speak with a stress management specialist. It helped me remember why I'd decided to come here. And when they offered me the chance to take a trip home, I answered with a resounding '*NO!*' I wanted to stay and finish what I had started, now that I didn't feel as stressed out."

Georgia had reinforced her success by remembering why she had joined the Peace Corps in the first place, admittedly with a little help. Do this now--make a list reminding yourself of the reasons why you moved abroad. Though your business might not be as selfless as Georgia's, her list looked something like this:

To be part of something bigger than myself

To make a difference in the world

To see parts of the world that nobody else I know has seen

To get an experience completely different from the one at home

To make a few really good friends from different countries

To come home with some incredible stories to tell

At least a few of those will be on your list. Write it down. Print it out. Frame it. Hang it somewhere where you can see it daily. These little mantras will serve as vibrant reminders to keep succeeding.

But what happens when success is even harder to grasp? At some point in reading this book, you probably laughed out loud, "That's not me. I can't fix my situation that easily. It's hard to be an expatriate and impossible to live abroad." Moving abroad, or anywhere for that matter, is hard. That doesn't mean you should give up at the drop of the hat. But if you find yourself regularly thinking about returning home, it might be time to consider repatriation more seriously.

A Note about Repatriation

Expatriating is not for everyone. The difficulty of assimilation depends both on the country and on the personality type. Like holding on to a relationship for too long, sometimes host country and expatriate worker are just not a fit.

"I figured it out pretty early on," remembers Peter B., a senior project manager. "All hell broke loose in every possible way. There was constant drama with my daughters, who were miserable without their friends. I was woefully underprepared to deal with the language and general hygiene of the Turkish people and accidentally made myself an enemy at work. Okay, not completely by accident. But the damage had been done."

Repatriation Tip

If you plan to return to America with the same company, you will want to keep in touch with executives and colleagues throughout your expatriation. **Keep your network working on both sides of the ocean.**

Not everybody has the personality qualities for living abroad. The book *Workplace Warfare* discusses the four main personality types: Dominator, Influencer, Supporter and Curator. Half are people-oriented and half are task-oriented. Half are fast-paced and half are slow-paced. None of them is 'better' than the other, although our personal preferences will naturally gravitate toward one. You may be an Influencer who loves to connect with people in a fun, fast-paced environment. You may love to travel abroad and make instant connections with people across cultures.

But a Curator, for example, might not be able to make those connections as easily. Curators love structure and rules. For Curators, everything has a place and a purpose. Going with the flow is not their strong suit. If a flight gets cancelled or ground lamb turns up in their vegetarian meal, watch out! Spontaneity is a source of stress.

That isn't to say that Curators can't be expatriate workers. They may not be naturally inclined to those personality traits that seem ideal to organizations looking to find a suitable employee for placement. But their skill in remaining organized and showing up prepared could prevent a lot of heartbreak when it comes to expectations. They've done their research – they already know what to expect, the exact conversion rates, where their plane tickets are located, how much they'll have to budget for food and transportation each week, and although they may not be flexible in the face of adversity, they have backup plans.

The point is that everyone has qualities that could help or hinder them. Some just have more than others. In Peter's case of being challenged at work and at home, he could not resolve his interpersonal issues at the office and was not prepared to deal with his daughters' concerns. He accepted the fact that he had made a mistake and corrected it by moving home.

Don't buy in to hindsight thinking: "If only I hadn't moved away;" "If only I'd known more coming into it;" "If only I had had more of a voice in deciding on our residence." First of all, there's no way of knowing if any of that is true. Every decision we make comes with its own set of downsides. Second, in no way does hindsight benefit you in making decisions. If the past was a mistake, learn from it and then let it go. You still have every moment ahead of you to make better decisions in the future.

Repatriation is not a decision to make lightly. Take pride in the fact that you have been specifically selected for this assignment. Make a list of pros and cons. Will the regret outweigh the temporary discomfort you feel? Remember that most assignments are temporary and that this opportunity does not get handed out every day. Can you latch on to the positives of your experience (trying new things, learning to be spontaneous, meeting great people) to carry you through the negatives?

Sometimes, even moving back home can feel like being displaced again in a foreign country. You expect things to be the same, but your friends have moved on and you've changed, too. Your political ideas might have been influenced by what you saw abroad. You might have more tolerance for different cultures now, while your friends have started complaining about diversity. Maybe you even joined in with them before moving abroad. But now, you just don't fit in. You don't have shared experiences.

"I don't regret my decision to move back home," says Elyse L., an engineering consultant. "In the end, it was what was best for my kids. They had all kinds of attention and friends at school. It gave them an edge on all the rest when they started applying to college. But it was hard getting back in the swing of things. I had forgotten how cliquey and materialistic people here are and after our minimalist lifestyle in Costa Rica, it was really a culture shock. I found myself racing to keep up with the Joneses, getting back on the hamster wheel and every other metaphor you can possibly imagine. It all translated to the equivalent of losing my mind!"

You may have some golden, nostalgic image of what it was like back home. Remember that moving is tough, no matter where you're going. In the end, it will ultimately be up to you whether you move back to the United States or stick it out.

The term repatriation also refers to moving back after your assignment has been completed. Think of moving back home like moving abroad all over again. You'll have to get used to the culture, a culture that was at one point second-nature. You may be able to reconnect with friends and even make new ones based on your travels abroad. You'll have to plan for the logistics of packing up your belongings, selling or donating what you don't need and finding schools for your children again. You already traveled abroad once. No doubt you'll be able to do it again.

The Success Test

Are you succeeding? More importantly, is it even worth trying to succeed? This requires some thought. It's time to put you through your paces. Maybe a good old-fashioned 'pros and cons' list is in order. In lieu of that, more extensively, here are just some of the questions[18] to consider based on the success of some of the world's greatest philosophical leaders. Try to answer these questions quickly, as your gut reaction is usually the right one. These are all factors that you have direct control over:

---

18 Hill, "Think and Grow Rich."

The Success Test

1. Goal-Setting	**Yes**	**No**
Have you decided on a SMART goal in your life abroad?	☐	☐
Do you have a step-by-step plan for achieving your goals?	☐	☐
Do you easily see how your goals will benefit you in the long run?	☐	☐

2. Alliance	**Yes**	**No**
Do you have allies in your personal life and professional life?	☐	☐
Do you grant favors as often as you ask for them?	☐	☐
Do you have few recurring disagreements with others on certain subject matters?	☐	☐
Are you aware of the damage you can cause yourself and other employees by not cooperating with coworkers?	☐	☐

3. Courage and Fear	**Yes**	**No**
Are you confident in your ability to succeed?	☐	☐
Have you eliminated these six basic fears from your life?		
Fear of poverty	☐	☐
Fear of criticism	☐	☐
Fear of illness	☐	☐
Fear of loss of love	☐	☐
Fear of loss of liberty	☐	☐
Fear of death	☐	☐
Are you usually unafraid of the local culture?	☐	☐

4. Taking Initiative	**Yes**	**No**
Do you make a habit of doing more than you're expected to do at work or at home?	☐	☐
If you were an employer, would you be satisfied with the sort of service you provide as an employee?	☐	☐
Do you perform your tasks at work without needing supervision?	☐	☐
Do you ever create better plans for doing your work more efficiently?	☐	☐

5. Attitude	**Yes**	**No**
Do you feel in control over the aspects of your life?	☐	☐
Do you know how to detect a negative attitude in others?	☐	☐
Do you have a plan to cultivate a positive attitude when need be?	☐	☐
Can you put your enthusiasm to work in carrying out tasks?	☐	☐
Does your enthusiasm sometimes become the master of your judgment?	☐	☐
Are you eager to learn all you can about your job and surroundings?	☐	☐

6. Self-Discipline	**Yes**	**No**
In a heated discussion, do you speak before you think?	☐	☐
Do you 'keep your cool' in stressful situations?	☐	☐
Do you use good judgment even when your emotions come into play?	☐	☐
Do you concentrate all your thoughts on whatever you are doing at the moment?	☐	☐

Do you characterize yourself as "indecisive?"	☐	☐
Do you usually stick with your goals or assignments when it gets difficult?	☐	☐
7. Learning from Failure	**Yes**	**No**
Do you keep trying even after defeat?	☐	☐
If you fail in a given effort, do you begin again with a new plan?	☐	☐
Have you learned any lessons from defeat?	☐	☐
Do you easily see how defeat can be turned into an asset?	☐	☐
8. Creative Vision	**Yes**	**No**
Is your imagination keen and alert?	☐	☐
Do you make your own decisions or do you rely on input from others?	☐	☐
Do you often have creative, practical input at work?	☐	☐
9. Checks and Balances	**Yes**	**No**
Do you save a definite amount of your income?	☐	☐
Are you careful with your money on a day-to-day basis?	☐	☐
Do you get sufficient sleep each night?	☐	☐
Do you easily balance your spare time between activities?	☐	☐
How do you stay healthy?	☐	☐
Do you have go-to relaxation techniques when you're stressed?	☐	☐
10. Habits	**Yes**	**No**
Are you in control of your habits?	☐	☐

Have you eliminated undesirable habits?	☐	☐
In your work abroad, have you developed any new, desirable habits?	☐	☐
Totals:	**Yes**	**No**
	___	___

Add up the total number of "Yes" answers and the total number of "No" answers. Your total number of "Yes" answers reflects Successful Thinking. Did you get a high score out of 46 total? Congratulations! You are quickly becoming successful in your personal and work life, gaining confidence in yourself and in your foreign land. The number of "No" answers reflects Unsuccessful Thinking. If you got a high score, it might mean that you're struggling to fit in abroad. But don't fret if your "Yes" scores are low – there are still ways to fix what's broken. Your life is not made out of antique china – one slip and it's shattered. Failure in life can sometimes be much easier to mend. Congratulate yourself for your successful answers and then take a hard look at the ones that you didn't score well on and assess why.

An English teacher who took the test, Rob N., remarked, "It was startling to see how much I really believed in myself and how much I still had to work on. For example, I scored really well in section 5, but really poorly on sections 7 and 9. I had a positive outlook on everything except failure and my fear of failure was holding me back. I guess it was the perfectionist in me. My poor budget-keeping skills really didn't help, either." Rob ended up emailing his EAP for help and received both life coaching and practical budget-keeping tips. He had taken a few steps upward on the stairway to success.

What if you didn't score well in section 2, Alliance? There may be some things to do to get your interpersonal skills up to par. Recognize where you see areas for improvement. Maybe your coworkers always go out for dinner on Friday nights and you could offer to pay. Maybe you are always asking for someone to cover your shifts. Respond by offering to cover their shifts on late nights or long weekends.

If you need improvement on section 6, Self-Discipline, knowing this about yourself can be key. It will take a little work on your part, but try to stick with projects after they get hard. Reward yourself for taking positive steps in the right direction. Reinforce those good behaviors now and try out the Success Test again later. How did you do the second time around?

Chapter Three

You, Abroad

"One's destination is never a place, but
a new way of seeing things."
- Henry Miller

You are going to be challenged during your stay abroad. Your limits are going to be tested as you try new food, spend over your budget and encounter rude people. But you will also get a wonderful new taste for local culture, meet lifelong friends and return home with the experience of a lifetime. Some readers may even fall so deeply in love with their new, strange land that they build a permanent home there.

Obstacles are to be embraced. Mountain climbers understand this. Do they give up when the terrain gets a little steep? No! They dig in, dig deep, and try harder. They expect the way to be difficult from the outset, and when they reach the most difficult part of the ascent, they push themselves harder to reach their goal, the peak.

Single mother and newspaper editor Talia P. says, "Moving to Greece was always my dream. Maybe I rushed into it. I had no contacts there, barely knew the language and had little savings. But, I went with my six-year-old daughter and my dreams, found an English newspaper to work at and began to search around for schools.

"The trouble started when I went to a local school to figure out how to get Lise, my daughter, enrolled. I was battered with questions, interrogated stringently. *'Why are you here? Where is her father? Why isn't she in school?'* Nervously flipping through an English-Greek dictionary, I explained that indeed, that was why I was here, to get her in school.

"Once we were enrolled, the questions didn't stop. They called up once a week to ask me how Lise was doing and my daughter complained the teachers constantly separated her from the group and gave her remedial work to do." Talia shook her head, obviously frustrated at the mere memory. "I learned that Lise's teachers were tasked with making daily reports to the local Greek version of child services, to ensure that she was 'fitting in.' I was asked to submit to a home evaluation. I was told that my daughter wasn't fitting in, that I was a bad mother and that I should immediately take her back to the United States if I knew what was best for her."

When all signs point to home, take a moment to reconsider. Talia could easily have given up her dream, her new job and her new life in Greece to make the safer choice. But for her, that was not the definition of success.

In an article posted on her blog, Marian Schembari says, "Living abroad is what I imagine losing your right hand is like. You have to learn everything you've ever known all over again."[19] Then here's to being ambidextrous!

Talia added, "That's exactly how I felt. Completely up a river with no paddle and that river didn't seem to lead anywhere. So I asked my coworker if there was any way to address the issue. She said I was facing obvious discrimination and immediately sent me over an email address to an EAP, located right here in Greece. I explained my problem and they immediately sent me a list of legal services if I wanted to go that route, as well as a list of alternative schools in the

[19] Schembari, "Why I Wish."

area. I didn't want to get into a legal mess in Greece, but I did find a wonderful, two-room schoolhouse for Lise."

At that moment, her daughter ran into the background on the computer screen. "Mom! Can I go to Alex and Maris' house?" she asked in excited Greek.

Talia laughed. "Go on. Be home in time for dinner."

Expatriates have a unique opportunity to literally change the world, and not just in the touchy-feely sense. Zeeck studied and worked all over the world and finally landed a job in reporting and producing documentaries in India, Brazil, Spain and more[20]. He worked hard, eagerly taking on new tasks and interacting with the locals. But something was missing. Making friends and settling in was hard, especially when he had to move so often. So Zeeck and two friends founded InterNations, an online group with local, offline chapters around the world. "With InterNations, we wanted to make it easier for expatriates to interact, exchange information and ultimately make the best out of their life abroad,"[21] says Zeeck. As he traveled, he began to form local groups who could communicate with each other online, find great local restaurants and schools, and meet up for group activities like hiking and visiting museums. He saw a need, defined a goal and fulfilled it. Now, InterNations is the world's largest community of expatriates with a huge online and offline presence in over 390 cities worldwide.

Your story may end up much like Zeeck's, with unintended side benefits. You might have traveled abroad to advance your career, and ended up getting a new sense of the world in which you live. You may return to America not so much as an American, but as a citizen of the world. Becoming an expatriate can bring you confidence in new situations, and give you new faith in your own abilities. Taking the position that was offered to you may literally change the course of your life. The friendships you and your family make in other

---

20 Zeeck, "About."

21 C., "[Interview]."

countries can last a lifetime. Your world view will have become broader, and you will no longer be the ethnocentric materialistic American you once were. You will see new opportunities in your life, new options that you might not have considered before.

There's a funny thing about dreams, sometimes they come out of left field, from where we least expect them. We tend to see them as romantic fairy tales. We wait for a prince or princess to come sweep us off our feet and ride off into the sunset, to live happily ever after. But real-life dreams are different; they're filled with strife and there is no 'happy ending' because there is no ending. It is a constant quest for success and it's hard. But it's also wonderful, exciting, adventurous and a once-in-a-lifetime opportunity to boost your resume, make lifelong friends and get a taste of a new culture. Your dream can become a reality. As Walt Disney said, "All our dreams can come true, if we have the courage to pursue them." So muster up the courage to pursue yours, no matter which corners of the world they take you to.

Special Thanks to Contributor Deanna Smith:

Deanna Smith is a retired executive assistant living in Atlanta. After rearing twins while maintaining a successful career, she enjoys a life of adventurous leisure: hang gliding, fly boarding, disc golf, tennis, golf, biking, travel and yoga. She is passionate about poker, and has played in World Series of Poker circuit events for the past three years. Smith enjoys reading and writing, and volunteers at her local library. She plans to continue living the dream, splitting her time in future years between Atlanta and the island of St. Simons, Georgia.

Bibliography

"Americans Living and Traveling Abroad." U.S. Government. June 5, 2013. http://www.usa.gov/Topics/Americans-Abroad.shtml.

Association of Americans Resident Overseas (AARO). Aaro.org. (Accessed May 31, 2013).

Brown, Robert J. (June 2008). "Dominant stressors on expatriate couples during international assignments." The International Journal of Human Resources Management, Vol. 19 (6): 10181034.

Butler, Julie R. "Challenges Faced By Expat Women: Part 2." Escapefromamerica.com. http://www.escapefromamerica.com/2011/10/challenges-faced-by-expat-women/. (Accessed May 31, 2013).

C., Nyssa. "[Interview] Malte Zeeck, Founder of InterNations, the World's Largest Community of Expats." TheCultureur.com. March 12, 2013. http://thecultureur.com/interview-malte-zeeck-founder-of-internations-the-largest-community-of-expats/. (Accessed June 6, 2013).

Cartus Corporation. "2012 Trends in Global Relocation". Last modified May 2012. https://www.cartusmoves.com/docs/203940650250b8f4d3813582012GlobalTrendsSurveyReport.pdf. (Accessed February 7, 2013).

Clancy, Ray. "Immersion language learning gives native level knowledge, it is suggested." April 26, 2012. ExpatForum. http://www.expatforum.com/general-considerations/

immersion-language-learning-gives-native-level-knowledge-it-is-suggested.html. (Accessed May 31, 2013).

Clark, Ann D. Workplace Warfare: Break Through Bureaucracy and Love Your Job Again. iUniverse, 2013.

ExpatExchange.com. Burlingame Interactive, Inc. 2013.

EasyExpat.com. EasyExpat Ltd. 2013.

ExpatForum.com. MoveForward.com Limited. 2013.

Expat Network. Expat Network. 2013.

"Expatriate challenges: What are the biggest problems for expatriates?" Just Landed. http://www.justlanded.com/english/Common/Footer/Expatriates/What-are-the-biggest-problems-for-expatriates. (Accessed May 31, 2013).

ExpatWomen: Inspiring Your Success Abroad. Expatwomen.com. 2012.

"Family Matters!" AMJ Campbell International Relocation Survey.Expatexpert.com.http://expatexpert.com/pdf/Report_on_Key_Findings_of_Family_Matters_Survey.pdf. (Accessed May 31, 2013).

Forleo, Marie and Derek Halpern. "Beaten by Self Sabotage? Marie Forleo Shows You How To Fight Back." YouTube Video. Social Triggers, 2012. http://socialtriggers.com/self-sabotage-marie-forleo/. (Accessed May 17, 2013).

Future Expats Forum: Create an Untethered Life Overseas. Future Expats Forum. 2013.

"Global Relocation Trends: 2012 Survey Report." Brookfield Global Relocation Services. http://espritgloballearning.com/wp-content/uploads/2011/03/2012-Brookfield-Global-Relocations-Trends-Survey.pdf. (Accessed May 31, 2013).

Hall, Susan. "Think it, write it, do it: How affirmations can work for you." Health 21, no. 2 (March 2007): 166.

Hill, Napoleon. "Think and Grow Rich: Your Key to Financial Wealth and Power." Success Co., 2009.

Kim, Young Yun. "An Integrative Theory of Communication and Cross-Cultural Adaptation." SAGE Publications, 2000.

"Living in France: The New Mobility." Escapeartist.com. (Accessed May 31, 2013).

Lizurek, Daniel. "Your 'Success Profile' Questionnaire." FastProfits: Words that Sell. http://www.fastprofits.com.au/blog/your-success-profile-questionnaire. (Accessed May 31, 2013).

Napoleon Hill Foundation. http://www.naphill.org/.

Overseas digest: Living and Working Abroad Made Easier. Global Trends Media LLC.2011. http://www.overseasdigest.com.

Poelzl, Volker. "Living Abroad: How to Choose the Country Best for You." Transitions Abroad Magazine, July/August 2006. (Accessed March 23, 2015).

Relocation Expert. "How to Recognize Fraudulent Moving Companies." Move One. July 19, 2011. http://www.moveoneinc.com/blog/moving/how-to-recognize-fraudulent-moving-companies/. (Accessed June 17, 2013).

Reuters. "Saudi Arabia to punish men over Christian woman convert." Arabian Business. May 13, 2013. http://www.arabianbusiness.com/saudi-arabia-punish-men-over-christian-woman-convert-501370.html. (Accessed June 17, 2013).

Schembari, Marian. "Why I Wish Everyone Lived Abroad." Marian Schembardi. May 15, 2013. http://marianlibrarian.com/2013/05/why-i-wish-everyone-lived-abroad/.

Society for Human Resource Management. "SHRM's 2012 HR Trend Book". Last modified 2011. http://www.weknownext.com/docs/SHRMS_HR_TRENDBOOK_2012.pdf. (Accessed February 7, 2013).

TransitionsAbroad.com. Transitions Abroad Publishing, Inc. 2013.

Weichert Relocation Services. "Current Global Workforce Mobility Trends". Last modified 2013. http://www.wrri.com/External/wp-content/plugins/email-before-download/download.php?dl=762c283ee19783fdcafd45b3a9013186. (Accessed February 7, 2013).

Wiles, Louise. "6 Move-Abroad Challenges Most Expatriates Face And How To Overcome Them." 2009. Succcessabroadcoaching.com. (Accessed September 18, 2012).

Winn, Patrick. "Are expats America's laziest voters?" October 14, 2012. Post-Gazette.com.

Workpermit.com. SIA workpermit.com. 2013.

Zeeck, Malte. "About: Team." InterNations.org. http://www.internations.org/about/team.(Accessed June 6, 2013).

Printed in the United States
By Bookmasters